OSPREY
PUBLISHING

Crusader Castles in the Holy Land 1097–1192

David Nicolle • Illustrated by Adam Hook

Series editors Marcus Cowper and Nikolai Bogdanovic

First published in Great Britain in 2004 by Osprey Publishing, Elms Court, Chapel Way, Botley, Oxford OX2 9LP, United Kingdom.
Email: info@ospreypublishing.com

ISBN 1 84176 715 8

Editorial: Ilios Publishing, Oxford, UK (www.iliospublishing.com)
Maps by The Map Studio
Design: Ken Vail Graphic Design, Cambridge, UK
Index by Alison Worthington
Originated by Grasmere Digital Imaging, Leeds, UK
Printed and bound by L-Rex Printing Company Ltd.

04 05 06 07 08   10 9 8 7 6 5 4 3 2 1

A CIP catalogue record for this book is available from the British Library.

FOR A CATALOGUE OF ALL BOOKS PUBLISHED BY OSPREY MILITARY AND AVIATION PLEASE CONTACT:

Osprey Direct UK, PO Box 140, Wellingborough, Northants, NN8 2FA, United Kingdom.
Email: info@ospreydirect.co.uk

Osprey Direct USA, c/o MBI Publishing, PO Box 1, 729 Prospect Ave, Osceola, WI 54020, USA.
Email: info@ospreydirectusa.com

www.ospreypublishing.com

Dedication

For the class of 2004, Hertford College, University of Oxford.

Image credits

Unless otherwise indicated, all photographic images and line-drawings are from the author's collection.

Measurements

Distances, ranges and dimensions are given in metric values in this volume:

1 millimetre (mm)	0.0394 inches
1 centimetre (cm)	0.3937 inches
1 metre (m)	1.0936 yards
1 kilometre (km)	0.6214 miles
1 kilogram (kg)	2.2046 pounds
1 tonne (t)	0.9842 long ton (UK)

The Fortress Study Group (FSG)

The object of the FSG is to advance the education of the public in the study of all aspects of fortifications and their armaments, especially works constructed to mount or resist artillery. The FSG holds an annual conference in September over a long weekend with visits and evening lectures, an annual tour abroad lasting about eight days, and an annual Members' Day.

The FSG journal *FORT* is published annually, and its newsletter *Casemate* is published three times a year. Membership is international. For further details, please contact:

The Secretary, c/o 6 Lanark Place, London W9 1BS, UK

Contents

Introduction

The First Crusade

In 1096 a remarkable 'armed pilgrimage' set off from Western Europe with apparently ill-defined objectives. These included supporting the Byzantine Empire, which had, for two decades, being attempting to recover vast territories lost to the Muslim Turks in what is now Turkey, and with hazey notions of regaining the Holy City of Jerusalem from Islamic rule. By 1099 these aims had crystalised into the capture of Jerusalem and Palestine, closely followed by the creation of a series of so-called Crusader States in what are now parts of Turkey, Syria, Lebanon, Israel, Palestine and Jordan – a process which had, in fact, already begun. For a while many of those Crusaders who remained in the Middle East, and numerous others who followed in their footsteps, envisaged the continuing expansion of Crusader-held territory, perhaps resulting in the entire destruction of the Islamic religion and its replacement by Christianity. In the event the remarkable success of the First Crusade would never be repeated, and the warrior elite that dominated the four Crusader States of Edessa, Antioch, Tripoli and Jerusalem had to build ever more formidable castles to defend their territories.

Crusader castles and the fortifications of cities that the Crusaders once occupied conjure up images of great fortresses dominating the landscape, or walled cities defying the wrath of surrounding Islamic states. In reality, fortifications that were taken over, repaired, extended or newly built by the Crusaders who erupted into the Middle East at the close of the 11th century existed in a great variety of sizes and styles. Furthermore, most of the towering castles whose photographs illustrate histories of the Crusades actually survive in a 13th-century or even a post-Crusader Islamic form. Fortifications dating from the 12th century, when the Crusader States were still a significant military force, are harder to find. Some exist as fragments, walls or towers embedded within later castles or city walls. Others are little more than shattered ruins or foundations in areas where later powers felt little need to maintain such fortifications. The remaining examples have all been altered by later occupants.

The First Crusaders, who captured Jerusalem in 1099, came to the Middle East with their own established ideas about military architecture. For most of them a castle was a fortification and a residence, though several variations had already emerged. The 10th and 11th centuries had seen the development of sophisticated European timber fortifications, even in areas where good building stone was available. This may have reflected a lack of sufficient skilled masons, but it is important to note that, within Europe, wooden fortresses were not necessarily weaker than those of stone.

Although the Carolingian Empire of Western and Central Europe had not been noted for its military architecture, it had built 'royal forts' at strategic points. These had much in common with late-Roman forts, though some also included relatively tall and sturdy towers. Partly as a result of the Scandinavian Viking, Islamic Saracen and Magyar Hungarian raids during the 9th and 10th centuries, the imperial or royal ban on members of the nobility constructing

The donjon or main keep of the Cilician castle at Anavarza was added to the fortifications by the Crusaders between 1098 and 1108, before the castle was rebuilt by the Armenian kings T'oros and Leon II. (Gertrude Bell)

fortresses without authorisation gradually waned. At the same time the crumbling Roman curtain-walls of many towns were repaired.

Small rural fortifications, built in increasing numbers, became characteristic of 11th-century France, and it was here that the motte and bailey castle emerged as a distinctive new form. However, during the 11th century, formidable stone castles and towers or keeps also appeared in some regions which had until then been dominated by earth and timber defences. Further south, stone and brick had remained the traditional materials when constructing fortifications. Here there is evidence that some existing stone halls were strengthened and heightened to become prototypes of the tall, freestanding donjon tower or keep, which became characteristic of much 12th-century Western European non-urban fortification. At the same time there was increasing interest in using naturally defensible sites such as rocky outcrops. Fortified churches similarly became a feature of southern France, an area from which so many participants of the First Crusade would come. Normans would play a very prominent role in the First Crusade, and Normandy and the Anglo-Norman Kingdom of England were in some respects ahead of the rest of France in matters of fortification (see Fortress 13 and 18, *Norman Stone Castles*). In fact the Normans were particularly closely associated with the new motte and bailey style of earth and timber castle.

Men from Germany and other parts of what was then simply called The Empire also played a significant role, but slightly different traditions and new styles of fortification had been developing in their homelands during the 10th and 11th centuries. From the late-10th century onwards a carefully planned system of provincial fortresses had been erected to control newly conquered Slav-inhabited territories along the eastern frontiers. Yet another series of developments could be seen south of the Alps, in Italy. Here cities like Rome had tried to maintain the impressive fortifications inherited from the Roman Empire. Meanwhile the military architecture that emerged in several parts of the country during the 11th century was often technologically more sophisticated than that seen north of the Alps, probably because of the close cultural, political, economic and military proximity of the Byzantine and Islamic worlds, where the art of fortification was even more advanced.

The First Crusaders may have marched east with their own varied traditions of military architecture, but when they reached the Byzantine Empire and then the Islamic states of the Middle East they found themselves facing some of the most massive, sophisticated and expensive fortifications outside China. At this stage the Western European Crusaders were on the offensive, and very rarely felt the need to erect strong fortifications. However, as soon as they had carved out what are now known as the Crusader States, they began building and were influenced by the military architecture they saw around them.

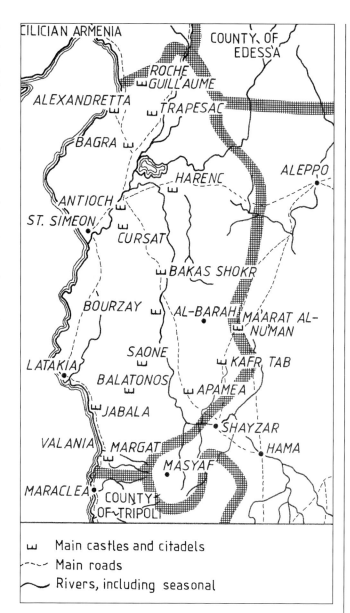

The Principality of Antioch, c.1137.

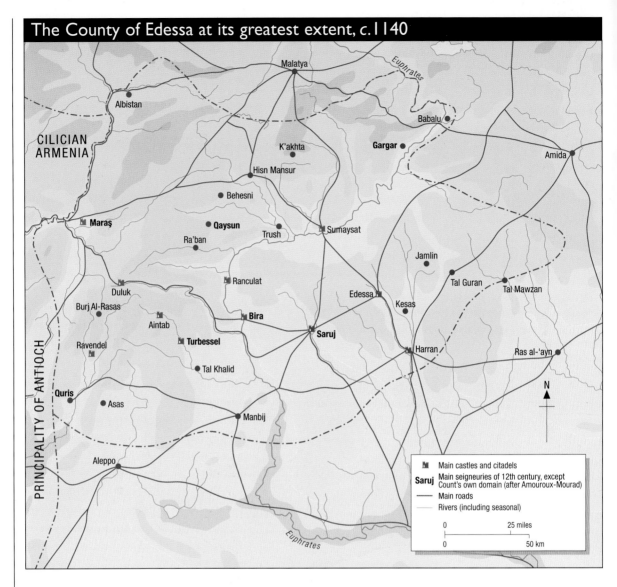

The County of Edessa at its greatest extent, c.1140

CILICIAN ARMENIA

PRINCIPALITY OF ANTIOCH

Albistan

Malatya

Euphrates

Babalu

Gargar

Amida

K'akhta

Hisn Mansur

Behesni

Maraş

Qaysun

Trush

Sumaysat

Ra'ban

Jamlin

Ranculat

Tal Guran

Tal Mawzan

Edessa

Duluk

Kesas

Burj Al-Rasas

Aintab

Bira

Saruj

Ravendel

Turbessel

Harran

Ras al-'ayn

Tal Khalid

Quris

Asas

Manbij

N

Aleppo

Euphrates

	Main castles and citadels
Saruj	Main seigneuries of 12th century, except Count's own domain (after Amouroux-Mourad)
	Main roads
	Rivers (including seasonal)

0   25 miles

0   50 km

The south-eastern bastion of the castle of Bile (Birecik) overlooking a crossing of the River Euphrates from the left bank of the river. Because of its strategic importance the castle includes elements from the Byzantine, Arab, Crusader and later periods. Most of what is visible seems to be Mamluk, though built on earlier foundations, with a roughly similar ground plan.

The Kingdom of Jerusalem, c.1160

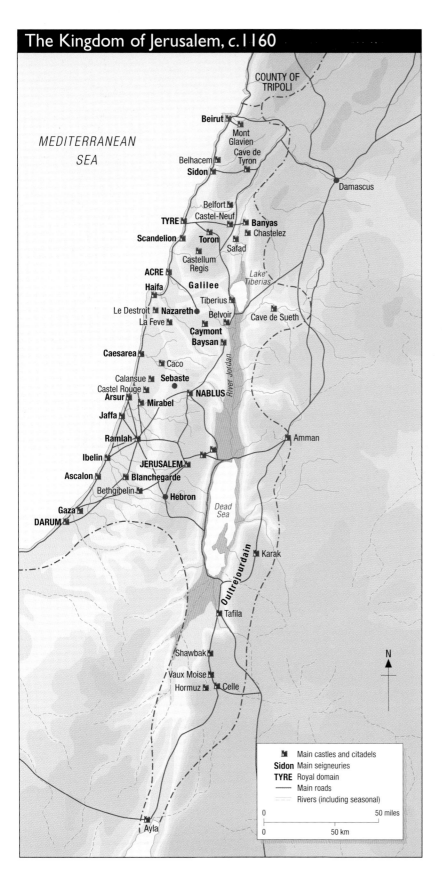

MEDITERRANEAN
SEA

COUNTY OF
TRIPOLI

Beirut
Mont Glavien
Belhacem
Cave de Tyron
Sidon
Damascus
Belfort
TYRE
Castel-Neuf
Banyas
Scandelion
Toron
Chastelez
Safad
Castellum Regis
ACRE
Lake Tiberias
Haifa
Galilee
Tiberius
Le Destroit
Nazareth
Belvoir
La Feve
Cave de Sueth
Caymont
Baysan
Caesarea
Caco
Calansue
Sebaste
Castel Rouge
Arsur
NABLUS
Mirabel
Jaffa
River Jordan
Ramlah
Amman
Ibelin
JERUSALEM
Ascalon
Blanchegarde
Bethgibelin
Hebron
Gaza
Dead Sea
DARUM
Karak
Outrejourdain
Tafila
N
Shawbak
Vaux Moise
Hormuz
Celle

Ayla

🏰	Main castles and citadels
Sidon	Main seigneuries
TYRE	Royal domain
——	Main roads
‑‑‑	Rivers (including seasonal)

0   50 miles
0   50 km

The Second Crusade

In 1144 Iman al-Din Zangi, the Muslim ruler of Mosul and Aleppo, reconquered the strongly fortified city of Edessa (Urfa) – the capital of a Crusader state (or County) of the same name. Zangi's success was the culmination of many campaigns in which the fortunes of war had sometimes favoured the Crusaders, and sometimes their Muslim rivals. Although the County of Edessa would survive in a reduced form for several more years, the fall of this, the first Crusader 'capital' city, sent shock waves across Western European Christendom and resulted in the Second Crusade. Unlike the First Crusade, the Second would be a massive, highly organised, military expedition led by European rulers of considerable power and status. It supposedly had the clear strategic aim of restoring the fortunes of the Latin Christian or Crusader States in the Middle East. This operation was on an unprecedented scale, yet resulted in total failure and humiliation outside the walls of the ancient Islamic city of Damascus. Here, the failure of the Second Crusade's attempt to capture what is now the capital of Syria shattered what remained of any Western European Crusader myth of military supremacy – at least amongst their Muslim neighbours.

Chronology

1096	Departure of the First Crusade for the Middle East.
1097–98	Siege of Antioch by the First Crusade.
1098	Establishment of the County of Edessa by Baldwin of Boulogne.
1099	First Crusade captures Jerusalem.
1100	Crusaders capture Sidon.
1101	Crusaders capture Arsuf; start of the Crusader siege of Tripoli.
1107	Crusaders capture al-Wu'aira in southern Jordan.
1109	Tripoli surrenders to the Crusaders after an eight-year siege.
1114	Maras is massively damaged by earthquake.
1115	Muslim army attacks Crusader-held Afamia; Muslim army takes Crusader-held Kafr Tab.
1115–16	Crusader campaign in southern Jordan.
1119	Muslim army attacks and takes the Crusader-held Atharib.
1124	Crusaders capture Tyre.
1129	Crusaders and Kingdom of Jerusalem attack Damascus.
1136	Frontier territory or March granted to the Templars in the Amanus Mountains of north-western Syria.
1144	Crusader-ruled city of Edessa retaken by Zangi; Count Raymond II of Tripoli grants the Hospitallers substantial territories around the Buqai'ah valley.
1147	Second Crusade is launched.
1148	Second Crusade defeated outside Damascus.
1151	Last Crusader castle in the County of Edessa surrenders to Nur al-Din.
1153	Crusaders capture Ascalon.
1157	Serious earthquake damages fortifications in north-western Syria.
1163–69	Five invasions of Egypt by the Crusader Kingdom of Jerusalem.
1170	Earthquake damages fortification in north-western Syria; Saladin captures the Crusader castle of Ayla.
1177	Crusaders defeat Saladin at the battle of Mont Gisard.
1179	Saladin captures and destroys the partially built Crusader castle of Vadum Jacob.
1183	Campaign by Reynald of Châtillon, Lord of Oultrejourdain, in northern Arabia and the Red Sea area.
1187	Saladin defeats Crusader Kingdom of Jerusalem at the battle of Hattin, retakes Jerusalem and most of the Kingdom of Jerusalem. His siege of Crusader-held Tartus is unsuccessful.
1188–89	Crusader castles in southern Jordan captured by Saladin.
1189	The Third Crusade begins. King Guy of Jerusalem besieges Acre, held by Saladin's garrison.
1191–92	Third Crusade retakes Acre. Saladin is defeated at the battle of Arsuf. Crusaders fail to reach Jerusalem, and agree a peace treaty with Saladin.

The County of Tripoli, c.1130.

PRINCIPALITY OF ANTIOCH · SHAYZAR · HAMA · MONT FERRAND · LA COLEE · RAFANEE · TUBAN · MARACLEA · TOKLE · FONTAINES · TORTOSA · CASTEL BLANC · HIMS · RUAD · CRAC DES CHEVALIERS · CASTEL ROUGE · TERRA GALIFA · COLIAT · ARIMA · LACUM · VILLEJARGON · GIBELCAR · TRIPOLI · CALMONT · RAISAGIUM · NEPHIN · MONTANÉE · LE PUY · BUISSA · BOTRON · MOINETRE · BAALBEK · GIBELET · BEIRUT · KINGDOM OF JERUSALEM

Main castles and citadels
Main roads
Rivers, including seasonal
UNDERLINED Main seigneuries
DOUBLE UNDERLINED Count's domain

Design and development

In the 19th and early-20th centuries, historians of the Crusades believed that Crusader military architecture was most strongly influenced by that of the Byzantine Empire. Shortly before World War I, a student from Oxford University conducted field research in the Asiatic provinces of the Ottoman Empire: he then returned to write a thesis in which he argued that the designers of Crusader castles largely based their ideas upon what was currently being built in Western Europe. This student's name was T.E. Lawrence, soon to be better known as Lawrence of Arabia. His thesis eventually influenced the next generation of historians of Crusader architecture, but neither they nor Lawrence seriously considered the influence of Islamic traditions of fortification. This idea developed more recently and today it is widely accepted that the military architecture of the Crusader States reflected a broad array of influences, in addition to the inventiveness of those who actually designed it.

The late Nikita Elisséeff, who worked for much of his life in Damascus, maintained that Byzantine forms of military architecture in northern Syria were soon added to the Western European design concepts of the early Crusaders. Within a few decades these newcomers were also learning from their Muslim neighbours, especially in making greater use of topographical features to strengthen a fortified site. More recently the Israeli scholar Ronnie Ellenblum highlighted the fact that Crusader castles were built to deal with specific military situations or threats, and that their designers drew upon what seemed most suitable in the circumstances.

In the early-12th century, each of the newly established Crusader states found itself in a different situation. The Principality of Antioch, for example, was adjacent to the Armenian states of Cilicia, which evolved into the Kingdom of Cilician or Lesser Armenia. Here fortifications ranged from tiny hilltop outposts to major garrison fortresses, while Armenian architects favoured half-round towers that protruded from a curtain-wall far enough to permit archers to enfilade the enemy. Such design ideas influenced castle building in the Principality of Antioch. Furthermore Antioch attracted few Western European settlers and hence relied to a greater extent on military elites of Armenian, Greek and Syrian origin who may also have influenced the design of local fortifications. The mountainous character of the Principality of Antioch and the County of Tripoli clearly encouraged experimental and daring design ideas, though the castles themselves ranged from very simple, almost rustic structures to huge hilltop fortresses. Meanwhile building techniques ranged from a typically Byzantine use of small masonry an bricks within one structure, to mixtures of Byzantine, Armenian, Western European and soon also Syrian-Islamic methods of both cutting and shaping stones – each of which had their own distinctive. Sometimes variations in ways of mixing cement and mortar also reflected different cultural influences.

Crusader castle building quickly grew more sophisticated. For example the building of concentric castles first took place in the late-1160s, and although the idea had been around for some time, concentric castles certainly appeared in the Crusader States before they did in Western Europe. On the other hand,

The rock-cut fosse and most of the fortifications of Edessa (Urfa) were completed before the arrival of the Crusaders. However the Crusader County of Edessa maintained these defences in a good state of repair and also carried out modifications. Note the rock-cut stone pier in the moat that originally supported a drawbridge.

At al-Wu'aira the builders of the Crusader castle widened and straightened an existing rocky gorge rather than excavating a fosse from the rock. The anvil-shaped outcrop in the centre of the picture was then pierced with a tunnel to make an outer gate. The stone steps and bridge that now link this rock outcrop to the castle on the right and the other side of the gorge on the left are modern. In the 12th century there would have been a drawbridge and a removable wooden bridge.

most early structures remained relatively small while the vast sums of money and effort expended on larger and more elaborate fortifications were characteristic of the 13th rather than the 12th century.

One 'supposed' characteristic of Crusader castles was a lack of timber in their construction, with this being attributed to a lack of suitable timber in the areas where they were built. However, abundant excellent timber was available in neighbouring Cilician Armenia. Although the deforestation of the Kingdom of Jerusalem may have been well advanced by the time of the Crusades, suitable large baulks of timber were available in the mountains of Lebanon and on Mount Carmel. The situation was better in the County of Tripoli, the Principality of Antioch and the northern regions of the County of Edessa. Furthermore Western Europeans probably enjoyed a technological advantage over their Middle Eastern foes, not only in their tradition of timber architecture but in their logistical ability to transport large timbers over long distances.

Consequently it is hardly surprising to find that in reality early Crusader castles made considerable use of wood. Timber roofs, floors, balconies, stairs, ladders and non-defensive storage buildings, barracks or stables were commonplace. Wood was also used for internal fittings, though these do not survive. Other evidence suggests that the newly settled Crusaders rapidly adopted local architectural traditions by being sparing in their use of timber, even in castles erected in relatively well-wooded regions. Of course, it was not simply the availability of wood that mattered: it was the availability of suitably large pieces of timber. Recent archaeological excavations at the unfinished castle of Vadum Jacob also show that timber was used for scaffolding and in other construction processes, though the builders did take advantage of alternative techniques where possible – for example the use of temporary earthen ramps to bring uilding materials to the top of a wall as it was being built.

During the 12th century, the experience of local builders skilled in the construction of substantial stone vaulting, broad arches, domes and other complex load-bearing structures became available to the conquerors: as a result, indigenous Syro-Palestinian architectural influence became more apparent in many aspects of Crusader architecture. In military architecture, the most significant developments were the placing of entrances beneath and through towers rather than through curtain-walls, the construction of defensive towers that protruded further from a wall to permit enfilading fire, and the use of a major tower or keep not as a final redoubt but as the fulcrum of an overall defensive scheme. Some of these concepts were rare or almost unknown in Western European fortification at the time. A further increase in the size and projection of towers, reflecting an increasing use of heavy counterweight stone-throwing mangonels would be a feature of the early-13th century. On the other hand the use of heavily embossed masonry as a means of making such missiles strike no more than a glancing blow was soon seen.

The inability of several Crusader fortifications to withstand enemy sieges became apparent in the 1160s and 1170s. Previously Islamic armies had relied on traditional methods of siege warfare, with direct assaults, blockades, mining and the limited use of relatively light stone-throwing artillery: although Islamic armies had access to superior siege technologies, a limited number of men skilled in heavy carpentry seems to have precluded the greater use of

sophisticated artillery. In the 1160s, however, things began to change and a process was set in motion that would eventually result in the Mamluk Sultanate's staggering number of huge timber-framed stone-throwing machines, which reached their peak in the late-13th century. Meanwhile the military setbacks suffered by the Crusader States resulted in the construction of bigger, stronger and notably more expensive castles. The owners of these new castles were not necessarily any richer, however; a fact which contributed to the rising military orders being asked to take over several castles because they were better able to garrison, maintain and defend them.

There was reduced reliance on a donjon and a greater emphasis on an enceinte or curtain-wall strengthened by towers. Yet there was also a tendency to increase the number of existing defensive features whilst shying away from incorporating new ones. Hence walls, towers, and fosse ditches were multiplied while the natural defensive features of a site were enhanced by excavation and what could almost be called 'landscaping'. Walls became thicker and the originally Islamic concept of the talus (an additional sloping front) along the lower parts of walls and towers was adopted. Ancient stone columns were added to walls as horizontal bonding, tying together the carefully laid outer and inner layers through a core filled with rubble and mortar. The number of embrasures for archery or observation was increased and single or superimposed horizontal defensive galleries, again with loopholes, became more common. Various forms of projecting machicolation appeared, which permitted arrows to be shot at, or missiles to be dropped on, enemies beneath. Both Byzantine and Islamic fortifications had, of course, made use of machicolations long before the Crusaders arrived. Meanwhile towers began to get bigger and more closely spaced, though the massive projecting artillery bastion towers of the early-13th century had not yet appeared.

The types of Crusader fortification

There were several basic forms of what can loosely be called Crusader fortifications. However, there was considerable overlap between them and no clear line of development even within these forms. The simplest was the free- or almost freestanding tower, an idea brought to the Middle East by the Crusaders. Single towers were found in many areas, most commonly in the more settled regions. The second was the castrum or enclosure within a fortified wall, usually rectangular with corner towers: these too were more common in settled areas. The double-castrum was a development of this simple castrum and could be seen as the earliest manifestation of the concentric castle: these tended to be built in more vulnerable frontier regions. Thirdly, the Crusaders used hilltop and spur-castles, the latter being sited upon a promontory attached to a hill by a narrow neck of land that could be cut off by a fosse or ditch. These were also common in unsettled areas. A fourth and characteristically Western Europe form of fortification has recently been added to this list: the motte and bailey castle. Originally of earth and timber, it was not previously thought to have been used in the Middle East.

A more sophisticated typology has been suggested by Adrian Boas who subdivides the towers into isolated towers, towers with outworks, and donjons as parts of larger castles. Castra are subdivided into simple castra, 'castrum and keep' castles that combined a castrum with a main tower or keep, and 'defended' castra with additional outworks. Double castra or early concentric castles, hilltop and spur-castles remained separate categories.

Towers

At least 75 tower castles have been identified in the Crusader Kingdom of Jerusalem alone, and they are far more numerous than small-scale fortifications from the pre-Crusader and post-Crusader periods. Although defensive towers had previously been attached to some earlier monasteries in this area, they were rare. Nor was there anything comparable in previous Byzantine, Armenian or Islamic military architecture. The majority of these Crusader towers date from the 12th century and while some were related to early feudal lordships, several were later integrated into more elaborate fortifications.

The castrum

The existing Islamic castra north of Caesarea were used by Crusader forces from the time of their arrival in Palestine. Kfar Lam was an irregular four-sided structure built of sandstone ashlar (stone cut into regular rectangular blocks) with round corner towers and additional towers flanking a gate on its southern side. Its walls were then strengthened with small external buttresses, and under Crusader occupation the gate was both narrowed and lowered.

The invading Crusaders soon built castra of their own in southern Palestine, supposedly to contain a perceived threat from Ascalon, which was held by

A selection of tower castles.
1. Casal des Plains, Yazur (after Leach).
2. Tal al-Badawiyah, basement (after Pease).
3. Khirbat Rushmiyah, tower with forebuilding (after Pease).
4–5. Bayt Jubr al-Tahtani, plan and section.
6. Turris Rubea, Burj al-Ahmar, first floor.
7. Turris Rubea, section Z–Z.
8. Turris Rubea, basement
9. Turris Rubea, section Y–Y (6–9 after Pease).

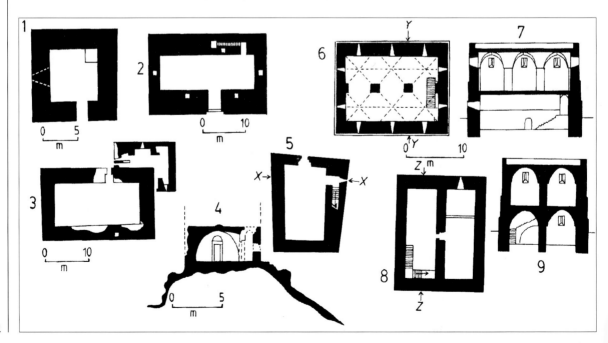

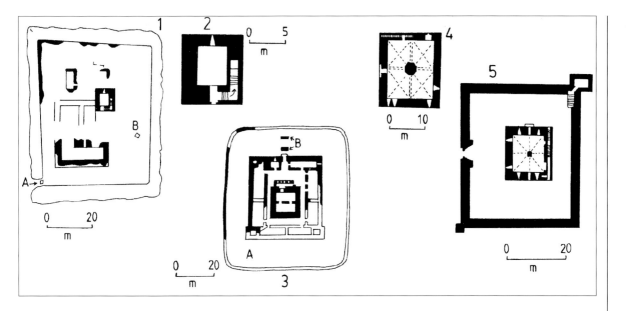

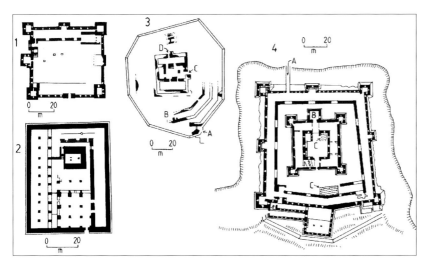

Fatimid forces until the mid-12th century. The example at al-Darum had one of its corner towers bigger than the others whereas those at Ibelin (Yibna) and Blanchegarde had four equal towers. Others in the centre and north of the Kingdom included Coliat, which was a simple castrum except that one tower was again larger and there were barrel-vaulted undercrofts along the northern and perhaps southern walls. The 'Sea Castle' at Sidon may originally have been a form of castrum, though it was later altered.

The Crusader castrum at Bethgibelin (Bayt Jibrin) was large and complex. It lies in a valley near freshwater springs and a road. Two main stages of construction have been identified. The first in 1136 used part of the existing Roman and Byzantine city wall and towers, strengthened with new wall construction. In the centre was an inner ward based upon an early Islamic Umayyad structure. When first built, Bethgibelin was described as a praesidium with a high wall, an antemurabilus (outer wall), towers and a moat. The ruins indicate an enclosure about 50m square with four corner towers, the entire layout being set inside the north-west corner of the ancient city walls. A second stage of construction saw the erection of outer walls and the excavation of a moat to create a larger defended area. This changed a simple square fortress into a complex concentric one. Both the inner and outer walls were strengthened with salient towers. The Israeli archaeologist Michael Cohen has recently suggested that Bethgibelin may have served as a model for future Crusader concentric castles.

Though one tower appears rather larger than the rest, there was no central keep at Bethgibelin. At al-Darum there was a dominant tower. Here the outworks were eventually strengthened and by the late-12th century included no less than 17 towers. Jubayl had projecting corner towers plus an additional tower on the eastern side of the north gate. Inside the courtyard was a keep, two storeys high with its entrance at first-floor level. This marriage of a castrum and a dominant keep seems to have been a significant advance in military architecture that could be credited to the Crusader States. The idea reached its full flowering at the Hospitaller castle of Belvoir, which was built shortly after 1168. It should also be noted though that some mid-12th century Islamic fortifications gave a dominant tower a more independent role in defence.

Hilltop and spur-castles

Crusader hilltop castles shared few characteristics other than their setting. For example, Judin (Qal'at Jiddin) in western Galilee consisted of two great towers enclosed by curtain-walls, with the massive eastern tower perhaps being the earliest. The entrance to this tower was at ground-floor level, leading to a passage within the thickness of the wall, which perhaps led to a latrine. A second door in the entrance passage led to a staircase to the first floor. Like the ground floor, this was barrel vaulted. Another staircase led from here to a second floor or the roof. The second tower at Qal'at Jiddin is unusual for such Crusader fortifications because it had three floors.

The spur-castles obviously shared certain features, principally in having the strongest part of their defences face a promontory that linked the 'spur' to the body of a neighbouring hill. Several of these spur-castles had a deep fosse or ditch cut across the promontory. However, some castles that were never occupied by the Crusaders, such as Shayzar, also had such rock-cut fosses.

Saone, in the southern part of the Principality of Antioch, is the least altered of the large 12th-century Crusader spur-castles. Here a tower keep was added to an existing Byzantine fortification before 1132 to dominate the curtain-wall with its smaller towers. The merlons of the crenellated wall are not pierced for archers

A selection of spur-castles.
1. Saone (Sahyun). (A) deep rock-cut fosse, (B) donjon, (C) Byzantine castle, (D) shallow fosse between upper and lower fortresses (after Deschamps & Müller-Wiener).
2. Saone donjon, ground floor (after Lawrence).
3. Saone donjon, first floor (after Lawrence).
4. Castellum Regis, al-Mi'ilyah (after Pease).
5. Arima (al-Araymah), probable early structures shown in black: (A) donjon, (B) main gate of inner citadel, (C) outer gate (after Müller-Wiener).
6. Burj al-Malih (after Conder).
7. Ravendel (Ravanda): (C) cisterns, (E) main entrance, (W) well (after Morray).

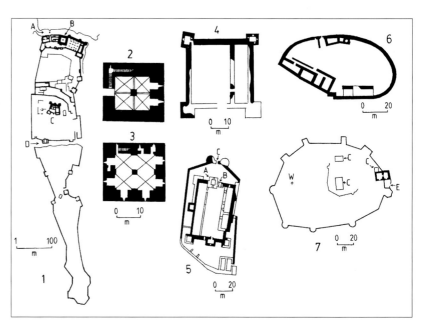

or crossbowmen though, as was typical of Islamic fortification, and most of the embrasures at Saone are also high up. Nor is there any direct communication between the keep and the curtain-wall, nor between some of the larger towers and the curtain-wall. These 'primitive' features might indicate residual Byzantine influence. Finally, the main tower at Saone is quite low, perhaps because it was built wholly of stone by designers who felt more comfortable using timber.

In 1031 the ruler of the Islamic city of Hims (in Syria) built a small castle at what was later known as Crac des Chevaliers. However none of this first structure has yet been found. Massively damaged by earthquakes in 1157 and 1170, Crac des Chevaliers was almost entirely rebuilt before being further extended by both the Hospitallers and the Mamluks in the 13th century, resulting in the magnificent castle seen today. Other than Saone, the oldest parts of Crac, 'Akkar in Lebanon and Karak in Jordan, the majority of existing spur-castles in what had been Crusader territory date from after the catastrophic battle of Hattin in 1187.

The rock-cut fosse that separated the spur-castle at Karak from the rest of the hill on the right is shallow compared to the example at Saone. This section of the outer wall dates from the late-1160s, while the structure behind is believed to date from the first Crusader castle, built around 1142.

Motte and bailey castles

Motte and bailey castles were typical of northern France and Norman England, while earthwork and motte fortifications were also seen in both northern and southern Italy. The man-made tals (or tells) that mark the sites of millenia-long human habitation in the Middle East already existed and were frequently used as centres of resistance, with or without formal fortifications on top: they were used in the same way as existing natural hills. More recently, Denys Pringle has identified at least one man-made motte in the Crusader States, on the site of the 'Land Castle' of Sidon. It seems to date from the 12th century but was largely destroyed during the construction of a larger castle in the 13th century.

Cave-fortresses

Ledge- and cave-fortresses are not usually included in the typologies of Crusader castles because they rely almost entirely upon their natural locations for defence, with man-made structures playing a secondary role. The only 12th-century ledge-fortress to have been studied in detail is near al-Naqa, not far from Petra in southern Jordan. This has been identified as Hormuz, the third Crusader fort in the Petra region, the others being al-Wu'aira and al-Habis. It is part way up a precipice which forms part of the Jabal Bayda mountain. For some time the ruins were regarded as the remains of a fortified 12th–13th-century Arab-Islamic village, but have now been identified as an isolated Crusader outpost facing west, across the Wadi Araba. Most other Crusader castles in southern Jordan were primarily concerned with threats from the east, north or south.

Crusader Hormuz consisted of about 15 rooms on the edge of a precipice. The walls comprised sandstone blocks from a nearby quarry and there was a gate through a narrow gorge or crack in the rock on the south-western side. Inside the site German archaeologists have found locally made Islamic pottery of a type also used by Crusader garrisons at other castles in southern Jordan. They also found millstones to grind flour. Water running off rocks on the upper part of the plateau was diverted into a cistern by a carefully constructed stone wall. Another round

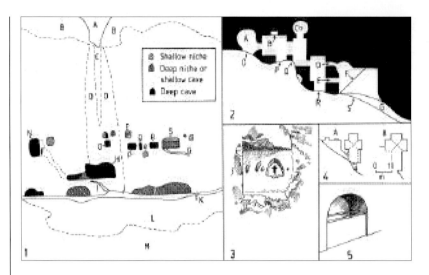

The Cave de Sueth ('Ain al-Habis, after Nicolle).

1. Schematic elevation of the main caves:(A) gulley, (B) steep slope, (C) dark water stain,(D) light water stain,(E) 'cross' niche, (F) approximate line of vertical mineshaft,(G) narrow ledge, (H) 'church' cave, (I) narrow ledge, (J) broad ledge, (K) grey stone wall,(L) vertical cliff,(M) steep slope, (N–S) third-level caves.
2. A plan of southern group of third-level caves based on verbal reports and external photographs: (A) possible plastered cistern, (B) tomb or ossiary, (C) font, (D) sloping tunnel, (E) sloping passage, (F) wall or step, (G) sloping ledge, (O–S) cave opening (see drawing 1).
3. The 'cross' niche.
4. Plans of the 'church' and remains of a neighbouring cave:(A) after Horsfield in the 1930s,(B) existing in 1987.
5. The ossiary or tomb based on verbal descriptions.

rock-cut cistern perhaps served as a filter pond, as its water then flowed into a larger catchment basin. Clearly the collection, retention and clarification of drinking water were of primary concern in such isolated desert outposts. The troops in Hormuz could control movement along the tracks that wound up from the Wadi Araba and Egypt beyond, while the larger garrisons at Karak and Shawbak could threaten the main road from Syria to western Arabia and Egypt.

Caves had been used as places of refuge from earliest times and were still used as centres of defence in the Middle East. For example, an underground church at Jumlayn in what became the Crusader County of Edessa has been fortified with a curtain-wall and ditch in the mid-11th century before the Crusaders arrived. A brief Crusader occupation resulted in no major changes, but what became the strategic castle of Qal'at Jumlayn (Çimdine Kalesi) was considerably strengthened after being taken by Islamic forces. In Lebanon the Cave de Tyron was used by the Crusaders as a simple fort, but little study has yet been made of this site. The most famous and best-recorded cave-fortress of the Crusader States is the Cave de Sueth in Jordan.

The Cave de Sueth

The Cave de Sueth, now known in Arabic as 'Ain al-Habis or 'Spring of the Hermit's Retreat', overlooks a gorge from the plateau into the Yarmouk valley. A seasonal stream forms an occasional waterfall down an overhanging cliff known as 'Araq al-Habis. The caves in this cliff were excavated as a hermitage or monastic retreat long before being used as a military outpost in the 12th century, when the Crusaders knew the site as the Cave de Sueth.

The history of this cave-fortress begins with the Crusaders' fortification of the lower Yarmouk valley in 1105. The invaders knew the area as the Terre de Suethe, from the Arabic word *sawad* meaning 'cultivated zone', in contrast to the semi-desert further east. That same year the area was ravaged by the ruler of Damascus, who also destroyed a new Crusader outpost on the Golan Heights. Instead of provoking further retaliation by building a castle on the Heights, the Crusader Prince of Galilee garrisoned the naturally defensible site of the Cave de Sueth on the southern side of the river, primarily as an observation post.

A peaceful arrangement lasted until 1111 when the Cave de Sueth fell to a force from Damascus. Two years later it reverted to Crusader control but in 1118 again fell to the Muslims before being almost immediately retaken by King Baldwin of Jerusalem. Thereafter the entire Yarmouk valley was held by the Crusaders, to be used as a base for further raids. Around this time another cave-fortress was established at Cavea Roob, probably near al-Mughayir or al-Shajarah 15km south-east of 'Ain al-Habis: here there are cisterns plus the remains of an associated medieval settlement.

Many of the surviving defences probably date from after Nur al-Din unsuccessfully besieged the cave-fortress in 1158. Wooden stairs, ladders and walkways almost certainly linked the three levels of caves, presumably being partially removable in an emergency. The Crusader chronicler William of Tyre described the Cave de Sueth as being set in a vertical cliff, inaccessible from

above or below and reached solely by a precipitous path across the mountainside. The caves, he said, consisted of rooms fully supplied with the necessities of life plus plenty of good water. It is even possible that the garrison was supplied with livestock stabled in the lower caves, which are still used by Jordanian shepherds.

Urban fortifications

The urban fortifications of the Crusader States were similar to those of neighbouring Islamic cities and, in fact, largely consisted of walls, towers and gates constructed before the Crusaders arrived. When these were repaired by the Christian conquerors, limited modifications were introduced, such as varied styles of stonework and the shape or position of new towers. Acre, for example, still only had a single circuit wall at the time of the Third Crusade. At Ascalon parts of the Fatimid defences included so much timber they they caught fire during the siege of 1153, which resulted in the city falling to the Crusaders. Almost 40 years later sufficient timber was available for Saladin to have the towers and walls 'filled' with wood and then burned down to deny them to the approaching enemy. At the smaller fortified coastal town of Arsuf the builders embedded their fortified wall in sand, as was also the case with several buildings inside the town. This may have helped the structures absorb earthquake shocks while also draining water away from the base of the fortifications. Furthermore a besieger would have encountered great difficulty trying to mine through sand.

Methods of construction

Until recently little research had been done on the techniques, materials, sources of timber and stone, and material transportation methods used in the construction of Crusader fortifications. Even less research had been undertaken into how fortifications were demolished or how materials from razed castles were re-used. It is unclear how early settlers from different countries enagaged their different traditions and experience in the building of castles, or to what extent they employed local labourers, skilled personel and architects. It is worth noting that several ancient building techniques were still in use in this part of the Middle East at the time of the Crusades.

The Cave de Sueth was a Crusader cave-fortress that made use of an earlier rock-cut Byzantine monastic retreat overlooking the precipitous valley of the River Yarmouk. Here the southernmost third and perhaps fourth level of man-made caves include two probable entrance points (centre-left) through which water from a seasonal waterfall was channelled into a cistern.

The cave-fortress of the Cave de Sueth under siege

The cave-fortress of the Cave de Sueth under siege

The Cave de Sueth was often raided, attacked or besieged, and fell to one side or the other several times. Unfortunately the site is also very vulnerable to earthquakes, and has suffered severe damage during its recorded history, both before and since the Crusader period. As a result most of the cliff face has collapsed into the deep valley of the River Yarmouk. Nevertheless, several man-made caves survive: some are still complete, others have only partial remains, and a few are only visible now as recesses in the cliff. Consequently the methods used to attach any outer wooden structures can only be guessed at, though the existence of such external galleries or hoardings is strongly suggested in various accounts of the Cave. In this reconstruction, a timber hoarding has been placed outside what appears to have been the most important caves in the complex, at what has been termed the 'third level'. Their openings led into what seems to have been a water-storage cistern and a series of neatly carved chambers that originally formed part of an Eastern Christian laura or monastic retreat. The timber hoarding or gallery itself has been envisaged as a smaller, more cramped and necessarily more flimsy version of the only complete and original timber hoarding to survive in Western Europe, which is located at Laval castle in France and dates from the 13th century.

One of the most carefully carved chambers in the cave-fortress of the Cave de Sueth was the church. It dated from before the Crusaders' arrival, when this site was a Christian monastic retreat. Today most of the front and one of the side-walls of the man-made cave have collapsed into the valley.

Three basic stones were available: hard limestone, softer limestone, and very hard volcanic basalt. Each had their characteristics and limitations. Normally Middle Eastern builders used what was locally available, stone only being transported long distances for a specific structural reason or for aesthetic considerations. Ablaq, the mixing of creamy white limestone and the darkest basalt, was a traditional form of decoration in Bilad al-Sham, the geographical and cultural area of Greater Syria.

Naturally the builders of castles, and those who paid the costs, tried to obtain suitable masonry from a local quarry or from the construction site itself. In the latter case, rock excavated from a man-made fosse or ditch could be used for the walls above. An estimated 17,000 tons of rock were, for example, removed to create the fosse at Saone. Similarly rock from an underground water-storage cistern beneath a castle or its courtyard might be used to build a tower above.

In naturally defensible sites such as hilltop or spur-castles, masons often shaped the rock to provide the walls with a firm footing. On other occasions they laid a shaped cement bedding. Considerable attention was given to providing good drainage systems to protect the foot of a wall and to collect drinking water. Existing rock formations could be used, or improved and then used, as buttresses. Other cracks or gaps in the rock might be integrated into the design, sometimes as a starting point for further excavation.

Though local stone was preferred for the bulk of a fortified structure, this was not always possible. Some local materials were unsuitable, at least for

The Cave de Sueth was accessed along a single path that ran across the sloping lower part of the cliff. Written records suggest that there was a gatehouse or wall at each end of the path. In fact four or five courses of dressed masonry are visible at the western end of the path, the lowest three courses consisting of dark grey stone that does not come from the immediate vicinity.

load-bearing parts of a building, and fine stone could be transported over substantial distances for structural or decorative purposes. The chapel at Belvoir is largely of fine stone whereas the rest of the castle is almost entirely of roughly hewn basalt from the surrounding ditch. Basalt, being extremely hard, is difficult to cut into complex shapes.

Most attention has focussed on the finely built castles of the central and northern regions of the Crusader States. However, many other fortifications were erected with remarkable speed and little apparent expense. The most obvious examples are those in the virtually autonomous province of Oultrejourdain: al-Salt, Karak, Tafila, Shawbak, Hormuz, Celle (al-Habis), Vaux Moise (al-Wu'aira) and Ayla (now believed to be on the Egyptian Sinai island of Jazirat Fara'un). This line of castles was built with limited money and labour, using rubble, ancient Nabatean masonry and a minimal amount of newly dressed stone. Refinement, it seems, was not considered necessary whereas the provision of reliable sources of water was much more significant

The re-use of existing materials from destroyed buildings was widespread: the insertion of antique columns as a form of horizontal bonding, noted previously, was already a characteristic of Islamic fortifications. The Crusader attitude to such matters was summed up by the chronicler William of Tyre when he described the building of Ibelin (Yibna) in 1144: 'First of all they laid the foundations, then they made four towers. Stones were to be found in sufficiency in those places where there had formerly been fortresses for, as they say, "A castle destroyed is a castle half remade".'

Middle Eastern architects traditionally tried to link stones together where the masonry supported vertical loads or the sideways stresses of arches. Otherwise, the use of dry-stone ashlar or finely cut blocks of stone without mortar continued until modern times. A less visible technique was the laying of horizontal ashlar across a wall, through a rubble core, to bind the entire structure together.

Some historians have pointed to the massive size of the blocks occasionally used in Crusader castles. However, this was little different from what was being done on the Islamic side of the frontier. Others have pointed to large rectangular blocks of stone with embossed centres as being typical of 12th-century Crusader military architecture, but these were neither universal nor limited to Christian fortifications. Furthermore, care must be taken with the idea that masonry with different surface finishes can distinguish Crusader and Islamic workmanship. Both used a variety of picks, hammers, cold-chisels and axes with heavy, thick heads, sometimes with a straight edge, sometimes with a notched edge. Each gave a different surface effect, especially on easily

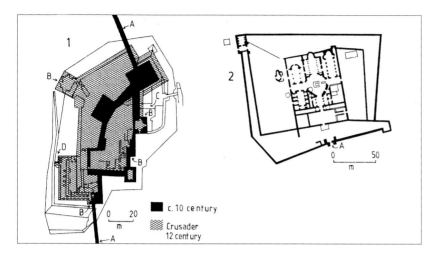

Urban and religious fortifications.
1. The Citadel of Jerusalem, known as the Tower of David: (A) city wall, (B) posterns, (C) inner gate, (D) outer gate (after Johns and Pringle).
2. The fortified Monastery of St Simeon (Süveydiye): (A) outer gate, probably from the Crusader period (after Djobadze and Morray).

worked limestone. However, Denys Pringle looked at the question in greater detail and wrote that ashlar bearing both diagonal dressing and masonry marks can almost always be attributed to the Crusader period while diagonal tooling and certain types of masonry marks are also found, though not together, on buildings of the Islamic Ayyubid period.

Where architects did not rely on dry-stone construction, various materials were used to tie the masonry together. The most common were various forms of mortar and cement, but other methods were also seen. For example, bitumen or petroleum tar comparable to that used to make modern roads was used to bind stones taken from an Islamic cemetery to make the Mahommeries Tower during the First Crusade's siege of Antioch. This apparently inflammable construction method was, in fact, more characteristic of medieval Iraq than Syria. On other occasions the laying of stone walls involved the use of metal tenons, cramps or pins, sometimes bedded in lead, a construction technique stretching back to the time of the ancient Greeks. It certainly made the resulting structure difficult to demolish, and there were references to its use in the Tower of David in Jerusalem, as well as in the fortifications of Maraclea, Sidon and Beirut. Perhaps it is worth noting that, with the exception of Jerusalem, all these sites are on the Mediterranean coast, the most Greek-influenced part of Greater Syria.

Skilled masons in the Crusader States included Greeks, Armenians, Syrian Christians and Western Europeans. Given the importance of such men and the vital need for fortifications one would assume that they would be well treated. However this was not always the case. According to one chronicler, Michael the Syrian, Count Baldwin II of Edessa began reconstructing the walls of Kesoun shortly before his death but treated his workers so badly that the work was delayed and, indeed, remained unfinished. The numerous slaves and prisoners of war who were employed in the construction of Crusader fortifications could not expect good treatment and are unlikely to have been entrusted with skilled work.

Recent excavations at the site of the unfinished castle of Vadum Jacob have shed remarkable light on how a 12th-century Crusader fortress was built. First the foundations were dug and the waste removed. Only then did building begin. Work actually started, in violation of an agreement with Saladin, about half a year before Saladin attacked the site. What happened next was described by Saladin's secretary, the Qadi al-Fadl:

The width of the wall surpassed ten cubits [about 5m]. It was built of stones of enormous size of which each block was seven cubits, more or less. The number of these dressed stones exceeded 20,000 and each stone, put in place and sealed into the masonry, cost not less than four dinars [high-

The building of the castle of Bethgibelin, 1136

value Islamic coinage] and even more. Between the two walls extended a line of massive blocks raised up to the proud summit of the mountains. The lime which was poured around the stone in order to seal it was mixed and incorporated into it, giving it a strength and solidity superior to the stone itself, and frustrating with more success than that of metal all attempts to destroy it.

The Qadi and other sources indicate that the site was well stocked with food, and the construction of a citadel was planned over a large water cistern. Many men were, in fact, still working on Vadum Jacob when Saladin attacked, including a hundred Muslim slaves and many horses. Islamic accounts of the

The Citadel at the highest point of the fortifications of the ancient city of Antioch largely dates from the Crusader occupation and includes both 12th- and 13th-century construction. The wall and early half-round towers seen here face inwards, towards the precipitous slope that runs down to the city below. In fact the upper line of walls lies on the crest of the mountain.

The building of the castle of Bethgibelin, 1136

Archaeological research has confirmed that the early Crusader castle of Bethgibelin (Bayt Jibrin) was built in two main stages, the most important work being done in 1136. The first builders naturally made use of surviving walls and foundations from part of an ancient Romano-Byzantine fortified city, but also added new walls (as the Crusader castle covered only part of the old city). The strongest or central part of the castle consisted of an inner ward based upon the ruins of another existing structure, this time an early Islamic so-called 'palace' or perhaps administrative centre dating from the Umayyad period. The second stage of Crusader building saw the construction of outer walls and a fosse that enclosed a

significantly larger area. The result was, by accident or design, a very early example of what became known as a concentric castle. Medieval building techniques and tools are illustrated in great detail in many manuscripts. They include wheelbarrows supported by a sturdy strap across the labourer's shoulders, hods, pallets, cold-chisels, special axes for smoothing stone, and masonry hammers. Walls were kept vertical and level with plumb-lines, and spirit-levels (which incorporated small plumb-lines rather than the 'bubble in a curved glass tube' used in modern examples). The items illustrated here are largely based on early 13th-century sources. The crane is powered by what was called a 'squirrel's cage', a surviving medieval example having been found in Beauvais Cathedral in France.

At least two stages in the construction of Karak castle are seen here. In the foreground are the remains of the walls and towers built during the second Crusader phase around 1168. Beyond and below it is a massive barbican dating from the Mamluk era in the late-13th and 14th centuries.

resulting siege state that the Crusader defenders lit fires behind the unfinished gates as a defence against sudden assault. In fact so much wood was piled up against the interior of the walls that the resulting fires caused the partially completed wall to crumble.

Archaeological evidence confirms several details of this attack. At the time Vadum Jacob consisted of half-finished walls and incomplete vaults, probably with wooden scaffolding in place. There were also several temporary walls, as well as piles of mortar and lime, dressed stones and earth ramps in various places. Around the walls were tracks hardened with layers of plaster where ox-carts could haul stone from a nearby quarry. Stone troughs to feed and water the oxen were placed alongside these tracks. There were earth ramps on both sides of the walls as well as large numbers of tools lying around. These included axes and chisels for cutting stone, spades, hoes, and spatulas for laying mortar and plaster. Inside one of the gates was a pile of lime with tools still embedded in it, as well as iron hubs that may have belonged to a wooden cart. Hundreds of arrowheads were found amongst these tools, showing that the defenders suffered hails of arrows.

On the northern, western and eastern sides of the site were small gates with stepped entrances, boltholes and beam channels for doors. Their purpose remains a mystery, since they opened inwards and would have been vulnerable to a battering ram. Perhaps they were intended for towers that had not yet been started. An artificial slope made of layers of rubble and soil probably taken from the interior of the fortress was piled against the sides of the castle wall. This slope was levelled and included several hard layers of lime. Oxen presumably hauled stones across this reinforced surface to the base of the wall from where the stones were lifted into position. Perhaps the builders intended to leave the material of the outer slopes as the basis of a later talus, or the material could have been intended to raise the level of a proposed outer bailey. Material piled against the inner side of the walls raised the ground level during construction, thus minimising the use of scarce timber for scaffolding though scaffolding remained necessary higher up. Timber formers were similarly needed during the constructing of barrel vaults, which were initially laid upon a half-wheel framework set into holes in the upper parts of the wall.

The principles of defence

The first line of defence for a castle or fortified city under siege was a ditch. These moats or fosses ranged from a shallow excavation, sometimes down to sea level where the fortification was on the coast, to a huge gash cut across the spur of a hill or mountain. The Crusader States seem to have taken the existing Byzantine and Islamic concept of a rock-cut ditch to much greater depths and widths.

Beyond the ditch would be one or more walls strengthened by towers. During the 12th century many such defensive circuits were built with dimensions very similar to those used in the late-Roman fortification of Syria. These remained the norm during the early Islamic period when advances in siege technology largely focussed on anti-personnel weapons rather than machines to destroy walls or towers. Even the adoption of beam-sling stone-throwing manjaniqs or mangonels had more impact on the uppermost parts of a fortification whose function was to protect the soldiers manning the walls, rather than on the main structure of a wall or tower. As a result towers still averaged around 5–6m in width and projected 3.5–4m ahead of a curtain-wall. As in late-Roman fortifications, towers were normally placed at approximately 30m intervals, which was suitable for providing enfilading fire by archers and crossbowmen. Small towers of this type were also adequate for early forms of man-powered stone-throwing mangonels. Most urban defensive walls in the Crusader States were strengthened by rectangular towers, though rounded towers were occasionally seen, as were a few pointed or triangular towers.

The primary focus was still on gates, though these were rarely attacked, presumably because their defences were so effective. Such gates could incorporate a portcullis of iron or timber and iron, which was raised and lowered along grooves in the side walls, as well as a drawbridge which normally would be raised by chains. Interestingly enough, the portcullis does not seem to have been favoured by Byzantine and Islamic military architects, even though it had been used by the Romans. Further protection was provided by panels in the gates, and embrasures in the side walls and roofs of gateways through which archers or crossbowmen could shoot at the enemy. During the 12th century the gates of Crusader-ruled cities were either flanked by towers or went beneath large towers or bastions. Posterns or postern gates were smaller openings in the outer defences. Their primary purpose was to enable defenders to attack the flanks of any enemy troops that came too close to the walls. They would presumably also enable messengers to come and go in relative secrecy, as well as permitting small numbers of fugitives or relieving troops to enter a fortress.

At this stage, stone-throwing mangonels were more effective in defensive than offensive siege warfare. However, the late-12th century saw early forms of counterweight mangonel enter more widespread use. The earliest clear account of such a weapon, in a book written for Saladin by Murda al-Tarsusi, stated that it needed a hole or trench through which its counterweight could swing. This problem was later overcome by raising the height of the frame. However, an otherwise unexplained trench still exists in the summit of the largest tower of the French castle of Bressuire, which probably dates from the late-12th or early-13th century – after the Plantagenet ruler of south-western France, King Richard the Lionhearted of England, had returned from Crusade.

The oval-shaped open water cistern near the Crusader Citadel at the summit of the fortifications of Antioch. The retaining wall would originally have gone all the way around.

Apart from stone-throwing machines, the main form of active defence in Crusader castles was archery. The latter not only included hand-drawn bows, mostly of composite construction like those used by neighbouring Islamic and Byzantine armies, but also crossbows. The effectiveness of defensive archery, if the fortifications had an adequate garrison, could be impressive. The chronicler Baha al-Din said that the Hospitaller castle of Belvoir was so actively defended that no Muslim besieger could 'appear at the entrance of his tent without putting on his armour'.

Archery was usually employed from the tops of the walls and towers that were crenellated, sometimes with pierced stone merlons through which an archer or crossbowman could shoot in relative safety. Other embrasures in the sides of walls and towers offered even better protection though their arcs of fire were necessarily limited. Stone machicolations enabled defenders to shoot vertically upon an enemy or drop rocks, heated sand or boiling water upon him. Heated oil and pitch were useful weapons against enemy siege machines made of wood, since they could be ignited by a burning brand or a fire-arrow. The simple stone corbels still visible at Saone and elsewhere show that some form of machicolation was used by Crusader architects in the 12th century. The structures supported by these corbels were probably of stone, though wooden hoardings (brattices) may have been possible. At Crac des Chevaliers the only square tower to survive in its original 12th-century form has three arched slot machicolations, above which lies a line of small

openings which probably gave access to a projecting machicolation added during the 13th century. A slot machicolation consisted of a broad groove down the face of a tower or wall, instead of a stone projection supported by corbels. It is also interesting to note that slot machicolations are seen at Château Gaillard in Normandy, built by King Richard I after he returned from Crusade (see Fortress 18: *Norman Stone Castles (2) Europe 950–1204* for a detailed study of this castle).

Many fortified walls and towers were provided with an additional defence against enemy mining: the talus. This sloping base increased the thickness of the structure but was not itself a load-bearing part of the wall or tower. Since 12th-century siege mining still focussed on attacking the base of a wall rather than sinking a mine and tunnelling beneath the fortifications, a talus served as an additional time-consuming obstacle whose collapse did not threaten the stability of the primary structure. The construction of double walls provided further obstruction to a besieger's progress, while also forming a 'killing zone' between the two walls until such time as the enemy took full possession of the outer defences. The inner wall and towers were built to a greater height than the outer ones, so that men on the inner defences could shoot over the outer wall and retained a height advantage if the outer wall was lost. Finally, the siting of the inner towers was usually such that they overlooked part of the outer wall between two of the latter's towers to provide a clear field of fire.

The castle of Gibelcar ('Akkar) lies to the left of this picture, which shows the remains of what was probably a rock-cut channel for water. The channel leads from a stream (in a steep valley that runs along the western side of the castle) into the castle. It was probably used to fill the castle's cisterns before a siege occurred, as it could easily be blocked by a besieger.

A tour of five Crusader castles

Given the wide variation in Crusader fortifications, no single example can be described as typical. A selection of five castles has been made here: Ravendel, Saone, Gibelcar, Belvoir and Le Vaux Moise.

Ravendel

Ravendel (Ravanda) castle was described by the Arab geographer Ibn Adim of Aleppo in the first half of the 13th century, after it had returned to Islamic rule. By then the castle had been repaired and strengthened but not greatly altered: 'It is a small castle on the top of a high hill, isolated in its situation. Neither mangonels nor arrows can reach it.' Ibn Adim had, in fact, highlighted the importance of location for this sort of relatively small castle in which a garrison could defy an enemy equipped with still primitive stone-throwing engines. Ibn Adim continued: 'It is one of the strongest castles, and most favoured spots. A valley runs north and west of the castle, like a fosse. It contains a permanent river.' Just as the author did in the early-1970s, the chronicler from Aleppo found the ascent far from easy: 'I made it up to the castle on horseback, but experienced great difficulty owing to its height, and the narrowness of the track to it.' The castle has a single curtain-wall on top of a long, steep slope. A short section of wall is doubled to form an angled rather than bent gate, to foil a battering ram. Some lower parts of the main wall and gate are made of irregular blocks of basalt with large spaces filled with mortar,

while the upper parts are of neat ashlar. In addition to arrow-slits there are still corbels, which once supported a brattice or machicolation above the gate.

The outer wall includes four rectangular towers, which project quite a way from the wall, and four rounded towers that do not protrude so far, plus a substantial polygonal tower next to the entrance. Inside the outer wall there is a large open area or enceinte around the remains of a much smaller inner wall with small rounded towers or salients that only project a short distance. Part of this inner fortification may date from the Byzantine or earlier Islamic periods. Within the inner wall are two cisterns while a third cistern is next to the main entrance.

Saone

Saone (Sahyun) is a far larger and more impressive structure, covering five hectares of a rocky spur about 25km from Latakia. The castle was virtually surrounded by steep cliffs except at the eastern end where a narrow neck of land, linking the site to the neighbouring hill, was cut by a stupendous man-made fosse over 155m long, almost 30m deep, and 15–20m wide. In the middle of the northern end of the fosse a needle of rock was left to support a bridge that led to a gatehouse in the wall.

This gatehouse had two projecting, rounded towers. The strongest defences were concentrated at this western end which formed a massive citadel dominated by a keep, just south of the gatehouse. On the other side of the keep were extensive vaulted stables, a cistern and three rounded towers. In the southern wall were large rectangular towers with a second gateway in the third tower from the east.

A chemin de ronde ran around the curtain-walls at Saone. This was not uncommon but at Saone the chemin de ronde has no access to the towers, which could only be reached by stairs from inside the courtyard, as was also the case with the walkway along the top of the curtain-wall.

BELOW During the 12th century the Crusaders extended the hilltop castle of Saone (Sahyun) in two directions. The western end of the spur on which the castle was built was enclosed by these relatively simple fortifications, as this part of the site was surrounded by cliffs and steep slopes.

LEFT The strongest parts of the fortifications of Saone castle were at the eastern end. These walls and towers, seen from inside the castle, overlooked the rock-cut fosse or ditch that separated the castle from the rest of the promontory.

The castle of Saone

The castle of Saone (Sahyun) holds a particularly important place in the history of Crusader military architecture because it was not recaptured after falling to Saladin in the wake of the Sultan's great victory at Hattin in 1187. Minor repairs and additions were made in later years, and these are clearly identifiable, the most obvious being a small Islamic palace, a mosque and a *hamam* or public bath in the centre of the fortified complex. By 1119 the existing small Byzantine castle (1) belonged to one of the great lords of the Principality of Antioch. By 1132 a massive though rather low donjon (2) had been added outside the existing eastern wall of the Byzantine fortified area. The most astonishing defensive feature, though, was a rock-cut fosse (3) across the neck of the promontory linking Saone to the neighbouring hill. The fortress eventually comprised an elongated walled hilltop, consisting of an Upper Ward (4) and a huge Lower Ward (5), separated by a wall and a shallow fosse. The defences of the Lower Ward were relatively weak. The strongest fortified structures were concentrated in the east, overlooking the great fosse, and to a lesser extent along the southern side of the Upper Ward where there was another strong entrance tower.

ABOVE LEFT The needle of rock that was left in place when the Crusaders, or more likely the slaves and prisoners of war forced to work for them, excavated the remarkable fosse at Saone. The fosse separated the castle, on the left, from the rest of the hill on the right, while the pillar itself originally supported a bridge.

ABOVE RIGHT The top of the rock needle in the fosse of Saone Castle. It is seen from the gate where a drawbridge would have been lowered onto the masonry on top of the pillar. A bridge would then have linked the pillar to a buttress-like extension of rock and the plateau beyond.

This was a feature of Byzantine castles, but was not generally adopted in later Crusader fortification. Nor can the multiple lines of Byzantine and Crusader fortifications at Saone be described as truly concentric, since the inner Byzantine defences are overlooked by the outer Crusader ones and were too far apart for mutual support. Another old-fashioned feature at Saone was a lack of arrow-slits in the walls, except for a few at the base of the towers. Consequently the walls of Saone had to be defended from their parapets. Most of Saone castle consists of what is now the Upper Ward, which contains the ruins of an earlier Byzantine citadel. A wall virtually cuts the Upper Ward in half while the western end of the site, separated by a second shallow fosse, forms the Lower Ward. This was probably not fortified before the Crusaders arrived, relying primarily on the precipitous cliffs for its security, but is now surrounded by weaker walls and small towers.

Gibelcar

Gibelcar ('Akkar) in Lebanon is one of the least-known Crusader castles. It stands on a narrow spur of land at the northern end of the Mount Lebanon Range with steep gorges on both sides and a view that is said to reach Crac des Chevaliers in Syria. Like Crac, Gibelcar is separated from the mountainside by a shallow rock-cut fosse. Outside this fosse a rock-cut channel once brought water to the castle. The fosse is dominated by a tall but relatively narrow tower keep. Otherwise the site is surrounded by a single curtain-wall on top of cliffs that, though not high, appear to have been cut away to make them smoother. Spaced around this wall are four rectangular towers. The towers, keep and parts of the curtain-wall were pierced by embrasures and inside the castle there was at least one cistern. The area within the curtain-wall was again divided into upper and lower wards, perhaps once separated by a trench. Sadly no recent archaeological work has been done on this dramatic and beautiful site.

Belvoir

In complete contrast to Gibelcar, the castle of Belvoir (Kawkab al-Hawa) has been entirely cleared and fully studied. In fact the Palestine village that once stood on this site was obliterated and its inhabitants expelled so that archaeologists could uncover the castle. It is surrounded on three sides by a rock-cut fosse, the eastern ends of which open onto a steep slope down to the Jordan valley. On the rectangular platform inside the fosse was a rectangular concentric castle largely built of basalt with some small decorative elements in limestone. It covered an area of approximately 100m by 140m with four rectangular corner towers plus slightly smaller towers in the middle of the northern, western and southern walls. The eastern wall, overlooking the Jordan valley, was protected by a large and slightly irregular barbican culminating in a substantial bastion. The main entrance was through the southern end of this barbican where the wall was doubled to form a long dog's-leg path before entering the main wall of the castle. In addition there were posterns through several towers.

Whether the multiple concentric plan of Belvoir was designed entirely for defensive reasons or partially reflected the fact that the Hospitallers were a monastic order who required a cloistered or enclosed area remains a matter of debate. The result was a strong outer wall with towers, then a large vaulted space that included storage, stables, a cistern and a large communal bath within a simple inner wall. These in turn enclosed a narrow courtyard surrounding a taller inner fortress with four corner towers and an even taller western tower over its entrance. The inner castle consisted of vaulted chambers including a kitchen, refectory, chapel and perhaps dormitories for the Brothers of the Order, surrounding a small inner courtyard.

The castle of 'Akkar in Lebanon, known to the Crusaders as Gibelcar, defied the First Crusade on its march south to Jerusalem. It fell later and became an important outpost in the County of Tripoli. Like many 12th-century Crusader castles it relied on an exceptionally rugged location rather than on its walls and a small keep, neither of which were particularly strong or sophisticated. Here the lower or northern end of the fortifications overlooks the 'Akkar river.

ABOVE At al-Wu'aira, the builders of the castle that the Crusaders knew as Le Vaux Moise used the natural location to maximise the site's defensive potential. Here, on the eastern site of the castle, one of the remaining towers and a crumbling stretch of curtain-wall overlook the near vertical gorge of the Wadi al-Wu'aira.

RIGHT The remaining lower parts of the south-western tower of the outer wall of the Hospitaller castle of Belvoir. Note that the sloping talus against the western wall (left) does not continue as far as the base of the tower itself because there is a small postern gate hidden in the shadow at this point.

Le Vaux Moise

Le Vaux Moise has now been identified as al-Wu'aira, a few kilometres from Petra in southern Jordan, where construction is generally believed to have

An embrasure in the largest surviving tower at Le Vaux Moise (al-Wu'aira) castle. Some features at al-Wu'aira are particularly important because they provide early examples of Crusader military architecture in a castle that was then abandoned, rather than being altered following the Islamic reconquest.

started after 1115. It consists of an irregular, four-sided fortified enclosure whose shape is largely dictated by the extremely rocky nature of the site. The outer walls stand on top of natural sandstone ridges overlooking water-worn gorges. The ravine on the eastern side of the castle was artificially deepened to create a highly effective vertical fosse, while a rocky pinnacle was left to support a bridge to the barbican and gate at the south-eastern corner of the castle. This is similar in concept to the amazing pinnacle at Saone, though much smaller, and has a tunnel cut through its top to form an outer gateway. The actual entrance to the castle was through a narrow rock-hewn passage near the southeastern corner, which was itself originally reached by a wooden bridge across the al-Wu'aira gorge.

The outer wall had several towers but the main bastions were the west tower, midway between the north-western and south-western corners of the castle,

The reasons why the designers and builders of the Hospitaller castle of Belvoir, on the western escarpment of the Jordan valley in Palestine, used black basalt and white limestone in their construction were practical as well as aesthetic. Here, in an arrow slit next to the south-eastern tower of Belvoir castle, imported but more easily worked limestone has been used for the complicated shape of a tapering arch, while black basalt forms the bulk of the structure.

The Hospitaller castle of Belvoir is perched on the edge of a steep slope dipping down to the Jordan valley, with the hills of Jordan rising beyond. Its designers thus only had to add a rock-cut fosse on three sides. The relatively shallow trench seen here is on the northern side of the castle.

plus the north-eastern tower which overlooks the Wadi al-Wu'aira ravine. Additional outworks strengthened the northern and southern walls. Within the walls, part of the floor of the enclosure was plastered with clay. Four finely carved white limestone blocks, two of which were decorated with Christian crosses, were inserted in the top course of the wall. They probably either came from a chapel built when the Crusaders first took over the site shortly after 1108, or from a pre-Crusader monastery. Other structures were placed around the insides of the main curtain-wall, leaving a large but irregular courtyard in the centre.

Feudal, religious and urban defences

Feudal tower building

For a while, during the Crusader 12th century, there seems to have been a castle-dwelling knightly aristocracy. When a piece of land was granted to a knight or group of knights in the newly established Kingdom of Jerusalem, many of these new fief holders did what was normal in Western Europe by erecting fortified towers or donjons. This may have been common during the optimistic first half of the 12th century; however, such an interpretation relies almost entirely on archaeological evidence since so few documentary sources survive. When feudal landholders later withdrew to the relative safety of fortified coastal cities, the knight or lord still sent representatives to supervise his fiefs, ensure the collection of rents, impose law and garrison local fortifications.

Towers built by the early feudal elite of the Crusader States varied considerably. Most had an outwork enclosing a courtyard around the tower. However, defence was largely passive and these fortifications were too small to house large garrisons. Some had halls that could have been used as administrative centres while others included large storage areas, perhaps for local agriculture produce. At the same time towers served as symbols of a new Crusader authority.

Most of the towers lay in fertile regions and their locations varied from flat land to hilltops. Some were very small, though even these could incorporate strong defences. One such tower was Mirabel, which was probably built in 1152. It had very thick walls plus outworks that included an enclosure with a sloping talus and towers. Most towers like this had walls with few openings, the towers themselves usually being two storeys high, which probably reflected weight problems with stone vaulting. Lighting was largely through arrow slits. Some towers also had machicolations above a single entrance, or a portcullis, or occasionally both. There was often a water cistern beneath the ground floor and some towers had latrines built into their walls.

Royal and large-scale castles

In addition to the practice of building small towers, the more powerful members of the new Crusader aristocracy took over, rebuilt or constructed new and more impressive castles. Qal'at Abu'l-Hasan (Belhacem), for example, was an Islamic castle occupied by a Crusader lord in 1128. It had two wards or open areas defended by a curtain-wall and rectangular towers. Like Gibelcar ('Akkar) in northern Lebanon, it stood on a rocky spur protected by a gorge on three sides.

In southern Palestine, the building of Bethgibelin castle initially seems to have been a local and communal affair in which the king was not directly involved. On the eastern side of the Dead Sea the castle of Krak des Moabites (al-Karak) was

The castle of Montréal (Shawbak) stands on a steep hill that, being in a broad valley, is lower than the surrounding plateau. Almost all of what can be seen today consists of the later medieval Islamic fortress, while the remains of a much smaller 12th-century Crusader castle are hidden within these massive walls.

founded by Payen the Butler, Lord of Montréal (Shawbak), in 1142. Far to the north, overlooking the Syrian coast, the first Crusader castle of Margat (al-Marqab) was built by the Mazoir family, but all that remains of their original castle is part of the curtain-wall with the rectangular towers. By the mid-12th century some feudal castles were quite large. At Montdidier (Madd al-Dayr) the donjon measured some 20m by 15m, with an outer wall enclosing a bailey about 60m square.

It might be assumed that royal castles would be larger than feudal castles and would be sited in more strategic locations. However, neither was the case. For example the first Crusader enlargement of the existing Islamic castle at Crac des Chevaliers was apparently carried out by Tancred as ruler of the Principality of Antioch. Montréal (Shawbak) in southern Jordan became the seat of the Lord of Oultrejordain, but the first Crusader castle was started in 1115 for King Baldwin I of Jerusalem. One of the most important features at Montréal was its water supply system, which reportedly consisted of a sloping underground tunnel with 365 steps leading to cisterns fed by underground springs inside the castle hill. It is also possible that the seasonal Wadi al-Bustan below Shawbak castle was irrigated by water diverted from other springs and there may have been water mills to process sugar cane brought from the Wadi Araba oases.

Although the Qal'at Sinjil Citadel overlooking Tripoli was rebuilt several times under Mamluk and Ottoman rule, much of the lower parts of its fortifications date from the Crusader period, perhaps including some 12th-century construction. The large chamber and embrasure seen here are in the ground-floor outer wall of a large tower on the eastern side of the castle overlooking the gorge of the Abu Ali River.

The Tower of David, Jerusalem

One clearly royal fortress was the so-called Tower of David, or Citadel, in the north-western corner of the fortified Old City of Jerusalem. It served as a royal palace until 1104 when the court moved to the Aqsa Mosque on the Haram al-Sharif, and was strong enough to resist a bombardment from outside and inside the city during a Crusader civil war in 1152. During the 1160s and 1170s the Citadel was strengthened with additional towers and and a curtain-wall to create a substantial fortified enclosure. Around 1172, it was described by Theoderich as being protected by ditches and outworks, while some decades later William of Tyre referred to its towers, walls and forewalls.

More is known about the organisation of royal than feudal castles. Naturally rulers tried to keep the largest and most important fortifications in their own hands. They also preferred to give the most powerful fiefs to their relatives.

The Hospitallers take over the castle of Turris Rubea in the 1190s

There were many reasons why castles and landed estates were handed over to the military orders by their feudal owners. Families might no longer feel capable of maintaining, garrisoning or defending such fortified properties; or they may have donated valuable assets to a religious order for the good of their souls. The death of the head of a noble family could, if he left no sons to succeed him, be reason enough. Turris Rubea (Burj al-Ahmar) had been given to the Abbey of St Mary Latina by 1158, and was then leased to the Hospitallers some time between 1187 and 1191, probably because of the virtual collapse of the Kingdom of Jerusalem following its catastrophic defeat at the battle of Hattin. In later years

Turris Rubea was in the hands of the rival military order of the Templars. Though not one of the biggest castles in the kingdom, it consisted of a fortified enclosure approximately 60m square that contained a massive donjon (1) plus other buildings. The walls of the donjon were over 2m thick and about 14m high. The basement or slightly sunken ground floor consisted of two parallel barrel-vaulted storage chambers (2). From here stairs ran up to an impressive hall, shown here, which seems to have consisted of six groin-vaulted bays with two massive central pillars. Lighting came from relatively narrow slit-windows (3), which were, however, too high in the walls to serve as arrow slits. Any active defence would have been conducted from the roof, though whether or not this was originally crenellated is unknown.

The Hospitallers take over the castle of Turris Rubea in the 1190s

These princely castles were under the command of châtelains appointed by the Prince or Count. Other châtelains were appointed by leading nobles. The importance of each châtelain reflected the importance of the castle he commanded. Meanwhile in cities and major towns other châtelains controlled the citadel and its garrison. In the Kingdom of Jerusalem a senior royal official called the Sénéchal (also called the Dapifer Regis) inspected castles in the king's name and organised their provisions. He had the authority to change garrisons but not the baillis or châtelains who commanded the castles since these were appointed by the king himself.

The fortification of religious centres

The military orders

The castles of the increasingly powerful military orders were distinct even in the 12th century. Most already consisted of substantial enclosure fortresses rather than simple towers, except for the simple fortifications that served as places of refuge and patrol bases along important pilgrim roads. The early enclosure castles of the military orders were usually rectangular with vaulted chambers around the insides of their walls, normally with a chapel, refectory and other conventual or monastic rooms in the upper floors over vaulted storage chambers and stables.

The Hospitallers seem to have selected more isolated locations for their castles during the 12th century than did the Templars. As a result more Hospitaller castles survive reasonably intact. Many guarded the Order's ever increasing landed estates. Perhaps a majority had originally been feudal castles handed over to the Order, along with large pieces of land, by families that could no longer maintain or garrison them. The castle of Calansue (al-Qalansuwa) was, for example, built by a local lord but was already in Hospitaller hands by 1128. The Order then added a hall and other structures to the existing tower. Bethgibelin was the second castle known to have been granted to the Hospitallers. The third was Belmont, a more elaborate fortress on top of a hill. It consisted of an outer wall without flanking towers, enclosing an area approximately 100m by 115m. There was a gatehouse in this outer wall while a vaulted passage ran around the inside. Within the enclosed courtyard was a rectangular inner bailey but no dominating tower or donjon.

The Hospitallers and Templars were also given castles and estates in the County of Tripoli before the middle of the 12th century. Castel Rouge was, for example, handed over to the Hospitallers by Count Raymond II of Tripoli while the castle's original owners, the Montopieu family, were awarded 400 bezants in compensation. The Hospitallers certainly put considerable effort and money

The tower of Castel Blanc (Burj Safitha) dominated the surrounding Syrian town. The 27m-high tower is a typical donjon and was rebuilt in the late-12th or early-13th century when it was occupied by the Templars. It is also one of the best-preserved Crusader fortifications in the Middle East. The ground floor served as a church, and continues to do so to this day. (Institut Français d'Archéologie, Beirut)

The military orders

Of all the military orders, the most significant were the Templars and the Hospitallers, at least where the Crusader States in the Middle East were concerned. Both evolved into clerical orders of militarised monks. Quite how this concept emerged, and how much it reflected the influence of religiously inspired military organisations outside the Christian world, remains a matter of scholarly debate. Each military order was also different, at least in its original functions, though most were similar in terms of recruitment, organisation and military role. The Templars seem to have been essentially military from the start, being dedicated to the protection of Christian pilgrims en route to various holy places early in the 12th century. The Hospitallers pre-dated them as an organisation, having developed out of a religiously inspired Latin Christian medical 'charity' in Jerusalem even before the arrival of the First Crusade. During the course of the 12th century these Orders took on increasing military roles, though the Hospitallers never abandoned their medical roots. The Orders also became rich and powerful as they received donations of money, land and castles. As a result the Hospitallers, Templars and other military orders proved better able to garrison and defend strategically important fortresses than even the rulers of the Crusader States themselves. They were also able to provide well equipped, highly motivated and constantly available military contingents.

into their holdings in the County of Tripoli after 1144 when Count Raymond granted them a virtually independent lordship in the east. This was a dangerous, yet strategically important area around the fertile Buqai'ah valley. Though blessed with adequate rainfull, it lacked natural defences and was very exposed to raiding. On the other hand, the Hospitallers' new estates in the Buqai'ah valley formed a useful base from which to raid Islamic territory, so the Order established its headquarters at Crac des Chevaliers.

By 1160 the Hospitallers had seven or eight castles in Syria, gaining a further 11 or 12 during the following decade. One of the strongest was Margat (al-Marqab), which lay within the Principality of Antioch. It had been the centre of the Mazoir family's extensive properties after 1130, but was sold to to the Hospitallers in 1186. At the same time the Order aquired various lesser castles and a patchwork of estates. Like Crac des Chevaliers in the County of Tripoli, al-Marqab in the Principality of Antioch developed as the military centre of what became a virtually autonomous palatinate.

The Templars' most important possession, and their headquarters, was on the Haram al-Sharif in Jerusalem – the site of the Temple of Solomon, from which they took their name. This stood at the south-eastern corner of the walled city of Jerusalem. A recently cleared tunnel near the south-eastern corner of the Haram al-Sharif was perhaps a 'secret' entrance to the Templars' fortified headquarters, used during emergencies.

The highly detailed Rule of the Military Order of the Templars does not make a clear distinction between a proper castle and an unfortified 'house' where brethren lived and administered the Order's estates. Both were under a commander in charge of all supplies and of the sergeants who guarded their gates. In fact the Rule of the Templars makes few references to castles or their role in warfare. By the second half of the 12th century most Templar castles were concentrated in the northern part of the Principality of Antioch and in the south of the Kingdom of Jerusalem. In the north these Templar castles formed a frontier march based upon Gaston (Baghras), Roche Guillaume, Roche de Roissel and Darbsak. In the south, some were close to Ascalon, which was held by the Fatimids until 1153. However, most Templar castles in the Kingdom of Jerusalem guarded pilgrim routes. They ensured that pilgrims had food, tents, animal transport and protection. One small Templar castle was Citerne Rouge, which defended a *caravanserai* or hostel on the road to the River Jordan. Another was Maldoim (Qal'at al-Damm), a four-sided fort built by the Templars before 1169 to protect the Jerusalem–Jericho road. It had a small tower with additional vaults and a strong rock-cut moat.

St Stephen's Gate in Jerusalem

The strongly fortified main gate in the northern wall of Jerusalem was called St Stephen's Gate under Crusader occupation. It was on the site of what is now known as the Damascus Gate, and in the previous Arab-Islamic period had been called the Gate of the Column. This had been defended by two large towers dating from the late-Roman and early-Byzantine periods, though it was later repaired and strengthened following various earthquakes. Water cisterns were built in front of one or perhaps originally both of these ancient towers during the early Islamic period. The city walls on either side also followed the old Romano-Byzantine line. The two ancient towers (1 and 2) were now incorporated into the Crusader gate, that on the western side now being strengthened with an additional lower wall. Most significant, however, were the new outer structures, including a third tower (3) near the existing eastern tower, which formed a small barbican (4) and a bent entrance that made the entire gate complex much stronger. Between the new and eastern towers was a large building, entered by stairs, which may have served as an administrative or customs post (5). The massive Umayyad period water cistern in front of the eastern tower was now beneath this (presumed customs) building, and it continued to supply the inhabitants of Jerusalem during the Crusader period. Next to the western tower and facing the 'customs' building was a small chapel whose interior was decorated with coloured plaster (6).

Religious houses and holy sites

During the 12th century Catholic Western-European religious houses were often fortified in the Crusader States. One was the convent of Benedictine nuns founded at Bethany in 1138. According to William of Tyre it consisted of 'a strongly fortified tower of hewn and polished stone. This was devoted to the necessary purpose of defence, that the maidens dedicated to God might have an impregnable fortress as a protection against the enemy.' In Bethlehem the Crusader occupiers even surrounded the Church of the Holy Nativity and its associated buildings with a fortified enclosure. This had strong gates and a massive donjon on its south-eastern corner, which might have contained the Bishop of Bethlehem's residence. The important Crusader site at Safita (Safad) may have been an *église-donjon* or fortified church. Here the central elongated rectangular tower was unusual, most other such keeps being almost square. Its outer defences included two outworks, an inner wall of uncertain shape and an outer polygonal curtain-wall with at least two towers and several vaulted chambers.

Urban defences

Most cities and towns of the Crusader States still had plenty of open spaces inside their fortified walls during the 12th century. These were used for market gardens and orchards. It was not until the late-12th and 13th centuries that the remaining Crusader-held cities along the Mediterranean coast began to fill up with settlers fleeing from lost territories in the interior. In fact several early-12th-century Crusader towns were not fortified, though they might contain a castle or fortified church, and within the Kingdom of Jerusalem only 14 towns had circuit-walls. Of these, 12 were walled before the Crusaders arrived.

Many existing walls, towers and gates were considerably strengthened under Western-European Crusader occupation, though mostly after the Third Crusade in the 1190s and during the 13th century. Their garrisons were drawn from a variety of different groups, especially during the first half of the 12th century. In the County of Edessa urban burgesses provided most of the non-noble troops who defended such cities. Many were Armenian. Unfortunately little is known about the troops who manned rural fortifications, though most were probably drawn from the European settler population or professional mercenaries.

The city of Jerusalem

The Crusaders' rebuilding of the walls of Jerusalem has been studied for over a century. It is clear that they not only re-used available masonry but also laid newly cut ashlar blocks. Shortly before the battle of Hattin (1187) the barons of the Kingdom of Jerusalem were obliged to pay for the reinforcement and

The Laqlaq Tower at the north-eastern corner of the walled Old City of Jerusalem. The First Crusade broke in west of this tower and during the 12th century their point of entry was marked by a large cross. Although most of the fortifications were later rebuilt during the Ottoman period, much of the lower part of the walls and towers incorporates Crusader masonry.

maintenance of the Holy City's fortifications. Nevertheless, the overall layout remained as it had been when the First Crusade arrived, with the significant exception of the greatly strengthened Tower of David Citadel.

By the time Jerusalem was retaken by Saladin's army, the area immediately outside the Citadel seems to have been enclosed within a network of fosses or moats, while a wall had been built within the riverbed which joined the north-western corner of the Citadel to a continuation of the curtain-wall. David's Gate (now called the Jaffa Gate) was rebuilt slightly west of its original position and was reconstructed as part of a new city wall. The original Fatimid tower in the north-western corner of the city was expanded by the Crusaders, who knew it as Tancred's Tower. Meanwhile a network of defensive ditches excavated in the 11th century along the north side of the city continued to function and may have been deepened. Here there were three gates, with St Mary Magdalene's Postern (Herod's Gate) being the furthest east. On one of the towers east of this gate there was reportedly a large cross marking the place where the First Crusade broke in to butcher the Muslim and Jewish inhabitants. In the centre of the northern walls was St Stephen's Gate (Damascus Gate), while to the west of this gate was a smaller entrance called St Lazarus' Postern. The most complex defences on the northern wall lay around St Stephen's Gate, which had an external and inner entrance, with an angled passage between them. The inner part of this gate included a chapel and what seems to have been a custom's post.

The eastern and western circuit-walls of Jerusalem were built along the lines of the ancient walls. The eastern wall had only one major entrance, the Gate of Jehoshapat (now the Lion's Gate). Less is known about the southern wall during the Crusader period, though it was perhaps a few metres inside today's wall. Here three gates and smaller posterns are known: the Postern of the Tannery west of the existing Dung Gate, the Zion Gate, and Belcayre's Postern. There was also a large tower built of limestone ashlar at the south-western corner of the city walls.

The Haram al-Sharif was also fortified. Its three southern entrances, now called the Double Gate, the Triple Gate and the Single Gate, were strongly reinforced by the now lost Templar's Wall, which enclosed them like a barbican. This contained an outer gate that was part of the structures adjacent to the southern side of the Aqsa Mosque. North of the Haram al-Sharif a quarter had been allocated to the native or Syrian Christians, largely consisting of people transferred from what is now southern Jordan after 1116. It occupied what had previously been the Jewish quarter and was protected by a new wall behind the Church of Mary Magdalene. This wall turned south-eastwards from the main wall to meet the eastern wall about 150m north of the present St Stephen's Gate, creating a double-wall defensive system in the vulnerable north-eastern corner of the city.

The fortifications of other cities and towns

Beyond Jerusalem, few other large inland towns boasted fortifications. Only Tiberius appears to have a proper circuit-wall. At Ramlah, the capital of Palestine in the earlier Islamic period, the Crusaders reportedly built a moated and fortified stronghold, but nothing now remains. At Nablus the only fortification from the Crusader period was a small tower serving as a place of refuge. In the other Crusader States to the north, Edessa was strongly fortified but its defences almost all predated the Crusader conquest. The same was true at Harran, where some impressive fortifications had been constructed around 1059, but the Crusaders were said to have rebuilt the structures thrown down by an earthquake in 1114. In Antioch, most of the fortifications are Byzantine, and although much of the Crusader Citadel survives, most of it dates from the 13th century. The town and defences of Tripoli were severely damaged in another earthquake in 1170 and had to be repaired in the late-12th or 13th centuries. At Jaffa the small port was only safe in summer; nevertheless its location as the closest port to Jerusalem caused the Crusaders to refortify the town immediately after they captured it.

Ports and harbours

Naval communications between the Crusader States and Western Europe were so important that considerable effort went into making the ports of Palestine, Lebanon, Syria and the Hatay province of Turkey secure. Several harbours were given special defence installations. Man-made harbours existed at Acre, Arsuf, 'Atlit, Caesarea, Beirut, Sidon, and Tyre, plus several others in the County of Tripoli and the Principality of Antioch. The towers built on the moles that sheltered open harbours also served as anchorages for booms across the entrances. Some could also serve as locations for anti-shipping, stone-throwing engines like those used in siege warfare. The harbours themselves were usually separated from the town by a fortified wall, though these were not as strong as the walls on the landward sides of these ports.

The walls and towers of the abandoned city of Ascalon were built on a largely man-made rampart, much of it of sand. Several towers dating from, or substantially rebuilt during, the Crusader period incorporate antique columns laid horizontally to bind the inner and outer layers of the walls.

The medieval harbour of Acre has been studied in detail. It had a mole and a quay, which were improved by Ibn Tulun, the ruler of Egypt in the 9th century. The sea level was two metres lower during the Middle Ages than today, whereas in Roman times it had been higher. Two maritime castles protected the entrance to the Crusader port. The first was the Tower of the Flies standing in the middle of the bay of Acre and commanding the south-eastern side of the entrance. First built in the Hellenistic period, it had several medieval layers, the

Bringing local produce into the fortified manor house of Aqua Bella, mid-12th century

Many though not all of the isolated manor houses that dotted the more fertile regions of the Crusader Kingdom of Jerusalem were fortified. Whether this was done for reasons of local insecurity, fear of enemy raiding or, as in Western Europe, merely because it was considered normal practice to fortify such buildings, remains unclear. They were, after all, statements of feudal power and authority as well as functioning farms and agricultural storage facilities. The manor house of Aqua Bella is one of the best-preserved in Palestine. It was perhaps built for a secular lord during the first half of the 12th century, but belonged to the Hospitallers by the second half of the 1160s. Built around a courtyard on quite a steep slope overlooking a valley, it was also close to the main medieval road between Jerusalem and the port of Jaffa. Part of the ground-floor level was cut into the hillside, with the resulting stone being used for the building above. In the centre was the roughly square courtyard (1) with an entrance on its eastern side. The three other sides of this yard led into barrel-vaulted chambers that would presumably have been used for storage or for the stabling of animals (2). The vault on the southern side (3) also included a press to make olive oil. A staircase on the southern side led to the upper part of the buildings, which included a chapel (4). Other vaulted chambers on this upper level probably served as kitchens, accommodation and additional storage areas (5).

The Citadel of Tripoli (Qal'at Sanjil) stands on top of a hill overlooking late-medieval Tripoli and the coastal port-suburb of al-Mina on the site of the early medieval and Crusader city. It was considerably modified by both the Mamluks and the Ottomans though its basic plan and inner keep are essentially Crusader work.

The only remaining sections of the seaward-facing wall of the city of Ascalon are in the south-eastern corner. Even here, around what was originally the Sea Gate, some structures teeter on the brink of collapse.

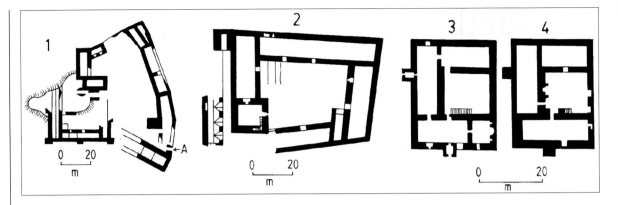

Examples of rural fortifications.
1. Burj Bardawil, a manor house:
   (A) gate (after Bir Zeit
   University survey).
2. al-Ram, a fortified grange
   (after Pringle).
3. Aqua Bella, a manor house,
   ground floor (after Pringle).
4. Aqua Bella, first floor
   (after Pringle).

earliest now being below sea level. This Crusader tower also served as a lighthouse for vessels entering the port. A second tower stood at the eastern end of the southern quay. Its remains are now a metre below sea level but it originally commanded the south-western side of the entrance to the port. A chain or boom protecting the port extended between this tower and the Tower of the Flies.

Fortified rural villages and houses

Before the Crusader conquest, most agricultural land in the Islamic Middle East was owned by *fallahin* peasants as freehold. However, this did not suit the feudal system introduced by the Western European conquerors, and as a result most of the indigenous peasants that remained became serfs while ownership of their lands transferred to the new Crusader aristocractic and settler elites. During the 12th century there was intensive Western European settlement, especially in the area north of Jerusalem. Here new towns, religious establishments, castles, towers and semi-fortified building complexes served as rural residences and granges or storage facilities for lesser Crusader lords and their vassals. In fact many non-military buildings in the Kingdom of Jerusalem included defensive elements, primarily because of the fear of raiding and of rebellion by the indigenous population. At the same time the inclusion of such fortified elements was traditional in many of those countries from which the Crusaders came.

In contrast, some new 'planned' Crusader villages consisted of buildings along a single main street, forming an elongated settlement that was difficult to defend: the indigenous villages of Palestine were settlements clustered around an open central area, with their outer buildings often forming a continuous defensive wall. Excavations at the Crusader village of Caymont (Tal Qaimun) show that the village was in places double-walled. However the fortifications were not strong, the outer being less than 1.25m thick while the inner was 1.50m thick. There were no towers in the surrounding wall though the village did contain one tower refuge. Another Crusader tower at al-Ram was later incorporated into a courtyard with surrounding vaults that included a wine press: Al-Ram has been identified as the grange of a 'new town' founded by the Canons of the Holy Sepulchre before 1160. In contrast, Forbelet (al-Taiyiba) is an example of a Crusader bovaria 'farm' in open countryside. It is a quasi-military structure built on Roman foundations but with no other defensive devices incorporated into its simple fortified wall.

Under Crusader occupation there was more intensive building in the rural regions of Palestine than at any other time since Umayyad rule in the 7th and 8th centuries. After the Crusaders were driven out, the construction work that characterised the Mamluk period focussed on cities and strategic fortresses plus roads, bridges and facilities for merchants or pilgrims: villages were largely left to their own devices and most small castles were abandoned.

48

The fortifications at war

The men who designed, built, garrisoned and attacked Crusader castles did so within military traditions that both inspired and limited their actions. Though the Crusader States were increasingly influenced by their Byzantine and Islamic rivals, their concepts of siege warfare remained rooted in their own Western-European heritages. During the 12th century the science of warfare in Europe was primarily focussed upon the taking and holding of fortified places including towns and castles. The possession of territory, rather than the fighting of unpredictable set-piece battles, was what normally won wars within this tradition. Another secondary but still important strategy was raiding and devastation as a form of economic warfare.

Under such circumstances, the defenders' primary aim was to limit damage done by the enemy and to attack the raiders' supply lines, or to assemble an army to attack these invaders while they were scattered. Risking battle was apparently considered more worthwhile in societies where fortifications were poorly developed, but this was no longer the case in Europe or the Middle East. Furthermore it is important to note that medieval Western-European, Byzantine and Middle-Eastern Islamic warfare all called for large numbers of military specialists or at least experienced soldiers. These would include garrison troops, artillerymen to operate stone-throwing war-machines, and engineers. All were normally included amongst the infantry and were further evidence that the idea of horsemen 'dominating' warfare during the medieval period is very misleading.

Strategic roles

Given the sophistication of 12th-century warfare in both Western Europe and the Middle East, it is not surprising to find that some castles or fortified places were given specific strategic roles. Reynaud de Châtillon, Lord of the virtually autonomous eastern fiefdom of Oultrejordain in the Kingdom of Jerusalem, decided to use his castles as springboards from which to extend his domination southwards into the Hijaz or western part of the Arabian peninsula. His strongly fortified lordship could, perhaps, also have been developed into an effective military barrier between the main Islamic political, economic and military power centres of Syria and Egypt. So it is hardly surprising that the removal of this threat, and of Reynaud de Châtillon himself, almost became an obsession for Saladin.

Further north the Terre de Suethe formed another smaller and more vulnerable extension of Crusader-held territory east of the River Jordan in what are now the Kingdom of Jordan and southern Syria. Here, for much of the 12th century, the garrison of the Crusader cave-fortress of La Cave de Sueth attempted to dominate the surrounding Arab villagers and bedouin. Their strong position at 'Ain al-Habis, overlooking the Yarmouk river, also enabled them to threaten the strategic road from Damascus to Arabia and Egypt.

An ability to threaten the enemy's communication from the relative safety of a castle offered several military, political and commercial advantages. For example, the Crusader castles in southern Jordan normally allowed Muslim pilgrims to use the ancient Haj road to the Islamic holy cities of Mecca and Medina in Arabia, but the Hajis or pilgrims often had to pay tolls. While the Crusaders held the so-called 'castle of Ayla', the same applied to Hajis travelling from Egypt across the Sinai Peninsula and the southern tip of Palestine. However, it is now thought that the Crusader castle of Ayla was on the island

Gaston (Baghras) near Antioch developed into a powerful fortress, though its greatest stength lay in its location on a rocky crag surrounded by cliffs. Here the builders of the castle did not even have to excavate a rock-cut fosse to separate the site from the neighbouring hill.

of Jazirat Fara'un rather than the mainland: this little island was recaptured by Saladin in 1170 and its fortifications were thereafter substantially enlarged. As a result there is, as yet, no clear archaeological evidence of Crusader architecture on Jazirat Fara'un. On the other hand, substantial Islamic forces, pilgrim caravans with adequate military escorts, and full-scale Islamic armies could cross such territories unhindered while the small garrisons of isolated Crusader castles dared not intervene.

In addition to threatening enemy communications, these Crusader castles could act as garrisoned strongpoints to secure the Crusaders' own lines of contact. This was considered extremely important, and the reason King Richard advanced so slowly towards Jerusalem during the final phase of the Third Crusade was his need to repair castles that Saladin had carefully destroyed along Richard's route. Unless these could be secured, the Crusaders could not be confident of protecting their extended supply lines. In the end the failure to secure the road to Jerusalem resulted in King Richard's advance failing, and Saladin retained control.

A tower or castle could also blockade a particularly stubborn enemy position. In such circumstances it was almost a case of 'castle versus castle'. This started very early in the history of the Crusades, with the erection of three strong towers during the First Crusade's siege of Antioch. The fact that two were built after the arrival of allied fleets on the nearby coast might suggest that they were made of timber from the ships in question, and perhaps also earth. In northen Italy tall timber 'counter-towers' were already a feature of siege warfare. However, the written accounts make it clear that at least one of these 'counter-forts', the Mahommeries Tower, was partially or wholly built of stone, despite the fact that it had been erected after the arrival of a Byzantine fleet manned by Anglo-Saxon exiles. Taking all the evidence into consideration it seems most likely that the Crusader counter-towers outside Antioch used whatever materials were available, be these stones from an Islamic cemetery, earth, rubble or timber from dismantled ships.

During the Crusader siege of Tripoli in 1101, the largely southern French or Provençal army of Raymond of St Gilles built a more substantial blockade castle overlooking the low-lying neck of land on which the port-city of Tripoli lay. This castle stood on a hill known to the Crusaders as Mons Peregrinus. It was subsequently called Jabal Sanjil in Arabic, or the 'Hill of St Gilles'. A small settlement soon developed around the base of the hill and in 1109 the Islamic port-city of Tripoli finally surrendered. This castle was extended considerably during the 12th and 13th centuries. However, the original city remained the main centre of population and it was not until after the Crusaders were expelled in the late-13th century that the ancient centre was largely abandoned and a new city developed around the castle. This became today's bustling city of Tripoli, while the old seaport declined into a sleepy suburb called al-Mina.

The Arab chronicler Ibn al-Athir seems to have regarded the Crusader castle of Mont Ferrand (Ba'rin) not far from the Islamic city of Hama as a sort of counter-castle or means of blockading Hama, rather like the castle built earlier to overlook Tripoli. On the other hand the well-known theory that several early Crusader castles in south-western Palestine were intended to contain raiding from Fatimid-held Ascalon is now widely discredited.

When used as bases for defensive operations, the castles of the Crusader States were often very well stocked with food and other supplies, not merely for their own garrisons but for use by a field army operating in the locality or camped close to the castle. This, according to William of Tyre, was the case with Artah and some other small neighbouring towns during 1119. On other occasions in the 12th century, the castle of Trapesac (Darbsak) appears to have served as a regional armoury or mobilisation store. Arima (al-Araymah in the County of Tripoli similarly seems to have been used as a storage base or distribution centre for military supplies during the mid-12th century. Fortified cities, of course, frequently fulfilled the same role, and the huge quantities of military material which fell into Saladin's hands when he conquered Acre in 1187 were surely not only for the city garrison's use.

The field armies that depended upon such well-protected stores did not necessarily have to win a battle to defeat an enemy invasion. In the autumn of 1183 the army of the Kingdom of Jerusalem successfully shadowed Saladin's invading force, first using Saffuriyah (Sephorie) and then al-Fula as secure bases. Eventually Saladin was obliged to withdraw, though only after ravaging large parts of the Crusader Kingdom. The castle of Saffuriyah was, in fact, an obvious place for the army of Jerusalem to gather if an enemy assembled around Damascus. Saffuriyah had plenty of water for a defending army as it waited to see if the enemy chose to cross the Jordan north or south of Lake Tiberius, both of which approaches could be covered from Saffuriyah. This was, at least initially, what the Crusader Kingdom's army did during Saladin's invasion of 1187. On this occasion King Guy's army camped about 1km south of Saffuriyah, around the largest springs in the area. However, Guy decided that a passive strategy was politically untenable and so marched to meet the invaders – resulting in Saladin's overwhelming victory at the battle of Hattin.

A place of refuge

If the Crusader States lost a battle, or felt unable to risk even shadowing the enemy, then their fortresses became places of refuge. After the defeat at Hattin, much of the Western-European settler population and those of its knightly elite who remained, were obliged to retreat into their castles, towers or whatever fortifications were available because the local non-Christian populations now rose against them. Some of these castles managed to hold out for a long time, and a few clung on until relieved by what developed into the Third Crusade. In most places, however, the remaining Crusader garrisons were seriously undermanned and perhaps demoralised. On the other hand, the established Middle-Eastern Islamic strategy that Saladin adopted (described in Shaykh

The rectangular donjon of Castel Rouge (al-Qalat Yahmur) seen from the north-east. A young student named T.E. Lawrence, the future Lawrence of Arabia, took this photograph before the outbreak of World War I. The donjon was surrounded by a wall with corner towers.

al-Harawi's military treatise for Saladin or his son) stated that a ruler should not unnecessarily court danger or even a setback. Instead a ruler was advised to mop up the weakest enemy places, thus maintaining the momentum of his campaign as well as the morale of his troops.

It was the intensity rather than the basic nature of siege warfare that changed during the 12th century. Certain features remained the same, the most obvious being a castle's physical location. In 1115 an Islamic army had little difficulty siezing the suburbs of Crusader-ruled Afamia, but their still primitive stone-throwing siege machines were unable to reach or damage the citadel of Afamia, which was on a high hill. That same year the Muslims attacked Crusader-held Kafr Tab. This time the same stone-throwing machines created a gap in the fortified wall – a remarkable feat given the small numbers and limited power of such weapons – through which infantry could make their assault. Four years later Crusader-held Atharib was similarly attacked and this time the Muslims' stone-throwing engines 'deprived the towers of their defences and killed the defenders'. Here it is clear that the mangonels' primary role was to smash wall-head defences and thus clear the garrison from such walls or towers. It is also clear that the Crusader garrison of Atharib had intended to make an active defence. However, mining at the base of their walls led the defenders to surrender because, as William of Tyre put it, 'The townsmen, fearing that when the ramparts were undermined the whole fortress would collapse headlong, surrendered the place.'

La Cave de Sueth

Another interesting and well-recorded siege was that of the Cave de Sueth. In 1174 Saladin took control of Damascus, and as a result the Cave de Sueth now faced the same powerful enemy to the north and to the south. But it was not until June 1182 that the storm broke and the Cave fell to a small force commanded by Farukh Shah, Saladin's formidable deputy in Damascus. The fact that this cave-fortress surrendered after only five days led to rumours of treachery within the Christian camp, perhaps on the part of the garrison commander. Farukh Shah's mamluk troops were, however, an elite. William of Tyre also reported that the enemy mined vertically through the soft rock, thus forcing the garrison to surrender. In fact a roughly hewn passage still leads almost vertically from a second-level cave to one of the third-level caves (see page 16). It seems a big excavation for only five days' work but Syrian military miners were amongst the most respected of their day. Although the vertical tunnel only allowed access to the northernmost third-level cave, this was presumably linked to the more important southern group of third-level caves by external walkways.

Perhaps the psychological impact of this mining operation and a consequent threat to the garrison's water supply prompted a quick surrender. The question of water is clearly important. The waterfall of 'Ain al-Habis only exists following rain and was presumably tapped to supply one or more cisterns within the southern third-level caves. The siege by Farukh Shah took place in late summer, before the rainy season, so the Crusader garrison would have been relying on stored water. If the Christians damaged the cisterns or polluted the water before surrendering, this would be of even greater significance where the second siege of 1182 was concerned, with the Crusaders attempting to retake the Cave. Farukh Shah's seizure of the Cave de Sueth had been the opening move in a major campaign during which Saladin failed to capture Beirut but went on to conquer substantial territory in northern Iraq. Meanwhile, Crusader forces counter-attacked Damascene territory. Farukh Shah also died around this time, weakening Islamic resistance.

William of Tyre stated that the Crusaders now brought their own miners to help besiege the cave-fortress, cutting away rocks on top of the cliff, which others then hurled down the precipice. Flints in the soft rock damaged their tools but these were immediately repaired by yet other workers, the whole operation being defended by troops camped on the hilltop. This bombardment continued day and night, perhaps smashing the wooden walkways and eventually demoralising the Muslim garrison. William of Tyre's description seems remarkably accurate, for there are traces of what appear to be man-made excavations terrifyingly close to the lip of the cliff above the caves. Meanwhile other warriors ventured along a narrow path leading to a ledge across the cliff-face. There they skirmished using spears, swords, bows and crossbows with a garrison consisting of only 70 picked men. Such skirmishing presumably took place around walls whose remains can still be seen north and south of the lower caves. After three weeks the exhausted garrison surrendered on honourable terms. The Cave de Sueth then remained in Crusader hands for a further five years until the entire area was abandoned following Saladin's great victory at the battle of Hattin. Thereafter its military role apparently disappeared.

Vadum Jacob, Saone and Bourzay

Archaeological excavations have shed fascinating light on how the unfinished Crusader castle at Vadum Jacob was lost. Work on Vadum Jacob began in October 1178, the King of Jerusalem reportedly employing the whole army of his kingdom in its construction. However, the workers were attacked by Saladin in August 1179. The Crusaders gathered their livestock into an area inside the southern gate and hastily built archery positions inside a small gate to the east. Saladin's troops attacked from the north, east and south, setting fire to wooden doors in the gates and shooting an astonishingly dense hail of arrows at the defenders within. Mining of the northern wall probably took place near the north-eastern corner of the unfinished fortress. On 30 August 1179 Vadum Jacob fell and its garrison was slain. After this there was no further attempt to fortify the site.

Information from other sieges later in the 12th century adds further details about how such places were both defended and attacked. Following Hattin and the fall of Jerusalem to Saladin, the arrival of Conrad of Monferrat at Tyre inspired its people to refuse Saladin's terms and to defend their city. On this occasion, according to Ibn al-Athir, they strengthened the fortifications and 'dug the moats anew', which suggests that the fosse and perhaps even the wall had been allowed to fall into disrepair. Further north along the coast, Saladin suffered another setback at Tartus in July 1188 where the Crusader garrison's heavy crossbow balistas, mostly installed in the keep, foiled the besiegers.

Later the same month the fall of the massive Crusader castle of Saone was a great shock to the Crusader States. General Hackett investigated this siege in his

Saladin's capture of the unfinished castle of Vadum Jacob, 1179

Saladin's capture of the unfinished castle of Vadum Jacob, 1179

The siege of Vadum Jacob by Saladin's army in 1179 has provided historians with an abundance of information about castle building and siege warfare in the 12th century. Not only was the event well documented, largely from the Islamic side, but the castle was also abandoned after its capture by Saladin. No further work was done on the unfinished fortifications and it was left as a virtual time capsule. Tools and other pieces of equipment remained where the Crusader workmen had dropped them; walls, gates, doors, piles of finished and semi-prepared masonry, lime for mortar and all the other paraphernalia of the 12th-century building trade lay scattered around. Such items have recently been uncovered by Israeli archaeologists, along with evidence confirming various details of the siege as described in the chronicles. The whole army of the Kingdom of Jerusalem is said to have been employed in the construction of Vadum Jacob but, as Saladin's army approached, they gathered their livestock inside the southern gate, including the beasts of burden used in construction work. This was presumably regarded as the easiest part of the unfinished fortress to defend. Another position was hurriedly constructed in a smaller gate on the eastern side. Saladin's troops attacked from the south, east and north, showering the defenders with a massive hail of arrows and managing to burn the wooden structures in and around the gates. Mining was also started, probably against the north-eastern corner of the existing defences, and the castle was overrun on 30 August 1179.

Oxford University B. Litt thesis in 1937. Having himself explored the site, he identified what he regarded as 'dead ground' in the south-east, which, he suggested, provided a suitable jumping off point for an assault. The 12th-century Arab chronicler Imad al-Din certainly mentioned 'an angle of the ditch that the Franks had neglected to fortify', perhaps referring to the same spot though in medieval terms. Given the immense effort put into the construction of the Crusader castle of Saone, it seems unlikely that its designers would make such a fundamental error and the truth can probably be found in changes in siege technology over the previous generation or so. This was clearly a time of rapid development, with the adoption of more powerful stone-throwing mangonels, including those powered by the counterweight principle, as well as advances in the design of crossbows.

The Crusader garrison of the mountaintop inland castle of Bourzay similarly relied on their crossbows to keep Saladin's fully armoured assault troops from hauling themselves up the extremely steep slopes when they attacked. Here, in August 1188, a bombardment by even the latest mangonels was impractical, so Saladin used his army's numerical superiority and the length of the Crusaders' walls to wear down the garrison: he conducted a sequence of limited assaults in difficult places throughout the heat of the day. Once again, at Bourzay Saladin's siege tactics closely mirrored advice given in the treatise written by Shaykh al-Harawi. It is also worth noting that both Muslim and Crusader chroniclers sometimes tended to exaggerate the steepness of the slopes upon which some Crusader castles were built. The present author, having clambered up several very steep slopes, and tumbled down a few, knows that they are tiring rather than exhausting, even in the height of summer.

The roughly rectangular outline of the unfinished Crusader castle of Vadum Jacob was visible even before the site was excavated by Israeli archaeologists. It stood on a low hill overlooking a strategically important crossing point, the Jisr Ya'kub, over the River Jordan. The slopes of the Golan Heights lie to the left. (Israel Antiquities Department)

The fate of the fortifications

The first of the Crusader States to fall was the County of Edessa, the last fortress of which surrendered to Nur al-Din in 1151. Having existed for only a little over half a century, and its western regions having already been strongly fortified, few of the County of Edessa's castles had been altered by the Crusaders. Some were then strengthened by the Ayyubid successors of Saladin. This territory then became a battleground between the Mamluk Sultanate of Syria-Egypt, and the Mongol or post-Mongol dynasties of Iraq-Iran. Consequently its fortresses, fortified towns and cities were extensively strengthened if not entirely rebuilt, particularly by the Mamluks.

The Principality of Antioch endured for much longer. On the other hand the Principality lost the lands east of the River Orontes – over half of its original territory – even before Saladin virtually destroyed the Kingdom of Jerusalem further south. Consequently, few of the fortifications at Harenc, Ma'arat al-Nu'man, Afamia and Kafr Tab date from the short-lived Crusader occupation. Several large and strategically more important castles, lost by the Crusader States in the later 12th century, then served to defend what had become Islamic frontier territory. Some, like Sahyun, previously called Saone by the Crusaders, were subsequently involved in inter-Islamic civil wars.

Other (mostly small) castles that had briefly been held in the Syrian coastal mountains where the Principality of Antioch and the Country of Tripoli met, were taken over by the Isma'ilis during the mid-12th century. These Isma'ilis were a sect of Shi'a Islam who often felt more threatened by the Sunni Muslim rulers of the great Syrian cities of the interior than by the Crusader invaders on the coast. As a consequence they strove to maintain an armed neutrality between the Crusader States and the Islamic states, basing their power upon small castles that dotted their own tiny mountainous state, several of which had been built or rebuilt by the Crusaders earlier in the 12th century. One such castle was at Qadmus, which had been constructed for a member of the Crusader feudal aristocracy.

Other Crusader fortifications remained in Christian hands for much longer, even after being briefly retaken by Islamic armies. Saladin, for example, spent eight days supervising the careful demolition of the walls of Tartus and the part of the citadel that his army had managed to capture. His effort to make them indefensible in the future failed though. Having been unable to take all of Tartus's citadel, he moved on and the city was soon retaken by the County of Tripoli, and its defences were greatly strengthened during the 13th century. The castles of Oultrejordain, far to the south, were never regained by the Crusaders after falling to Saladin's troops. Most of them were then greatly enlarged and altered under Islamic rule. Even the small rocky castle of al-Wu'aira was reoccupied during the Ayyubid period, though its fortifications were neither altered nor extended. Under Ayyubid rule, many of the fortifications regained by Saladin were rendered indefensible rather than simply being abandoned. Jerusalem was turned into what could almost be called an open city, with the Citadel as the only fortified structure to be maintained and strengthened.

Visiting the fortifications today

The historian or visitor who wants to explore 'untouched' 12th-century Crusader fortifications will find himself exploring shattered ruins. If the enthusiast wants to find more than this, he or she will almost inevitably be drawn to some of the less accessible and mountainous, though not necessarily least populated, regions of what were once the Crusader States of Edessa, Antioch, Tripoli and Jerusalem.

As we have already seen, the names given to cities, castles, villages and practically every other feature of the Middle Eastern landscape have changed since the 12th century. They were also known by different names by different peoples even during the period of the Crusades, though their Arabic names were perhaps the most widely understood. In the list of alternative names given below, Turkish and Hebrew names only apply to those locations that lie within the modern states of Turkey or Israel. Major places such as cities commonly known by variations of their correct or ancient names retain these names in the text of the book and consequently are not included in the list. This is not, of course, a comprehensive catalogue of sites fortified by the Crusaders during the 12th century.

Medieval French or Latin	Arabic	Turkish or Hebrew
Aila	'Aqabah & Jazirat Fara'un	–
Aintab	'Ayn Tab	Gaziantep
Albara	al-Barah	–
Alexandretta	Iskandariyah	Iskerderun
Amoude	Khan 'Amudah	–
Anamour	–	Anamur
Anazarbus	–	Anavarza
Apamea	Afamiyah (also Qal'at al-Mudiq)	–
Aqua Bella	–	'En Hemed
Aradus	Ruad or Arwad	–
Arima	al-Araymah	–
Arsur (Apollonia)	Arsuf	–
Ascalon	'Asqalan	Ashqelon
Balatonos	Balatun (or Qal'at al-Mahalbah)	–
Belfort (or Beaufort)	Shaqif Arnun (or Qal'at al-Shaqif)	–
Belhacem	Qal'at Abu'l-Hasan	–
Belinas	Banyas	–
Belmont	Suba	Zoba
Belvoir	Kawkab al-Hawa	–
Bethany	al-'Azariyah	–

Medieval French or Latin	Arabic	Turkish or Hebrew
Bethgibelin	Bayt Jibrin	Bet Guvrin
Bethsan	Baysan	Bet She'an
Bira	al-Bira	Birecik
Blanchegarde	Tal al-Safiyah	–
Bokebais	Abu Qubais	–
Botron (or Le Boutron)	al-Batrun	–
Caco	al-Qaqun	–
Caesarea	al-Qaisariyah	Sedot Yam
Cafarlet	Kfar Lam	Habonim
Calansue	al-Qalansuwa	–
Casal des Plains	Yazur	Azor
Casal Imbert	al-Zib	Akhziv
Castel Blanc	Burj Safitha	–
Castel Neuf	Hunin	–
Castel Rouge	al-Qalat Yahmur	–
Castellum Beroart	Minat al-Qal'a	Ashdod Yam
Castellum Regis	al-Mi'ilyah	Ma'alot
Cave de Sueth	'Ain al-Habis (or Habis Jaldak)	–
Cave de Tyron	Shaqif Tirun	–
Cavea	al-Mughayir	–

57

Medieval French or Latin	Arabic	Turkish or Hebrew
Caymont	Tal Qaimun	Yoqne'am
Celle	al-Habis	–
Château de la Vieille	Bikisra'il	–
Château Pelerin	'Atlit	–
Châteauneuf	Hunin	–
Cisterna Rubea	Qal'at al-Damm	–
Coliat	al-Qulai'ah	–
Crac des Chevaliers	Hisn al-Akrad	–
Cursat	Qusair	–
Daron	al-Darum	–
Edessa	al-Ruha	Urfa
Emmaus	Abu Ghosh (or Amwas)	–
Forbelet	al-Taiyiba	–
Gaston	Baghras	Bagra
Gibelcar	'Akkar (Jabal 'Akkar)	–
Gibelet (or Byblos)	Jubayl	–
Harenc	Harim	–
Hormuz	al-Naqa II	–
Ibelin	Yibna	Yavne
Judin	Qal'at Jiddin	–
Kadmos	Qadmus	–
Krak des Moabites	al-Karak	–
La Forbie	Harbiyah	–
La Tor de l'Opital	Burj al-Shamali	–
Le Destroit	Bab al-Ajal	–
Le Petit Gerin	Zirrin	–
Le Toron des Chevaliers	al-Atrun	–
Le Vaux Moise	al-Wu'aira	–

Medieval French or Latin	Arabic	Turkish or Hebrew
Maldoim	Qal'at al-Damm	–
Maraclea	Maraqiyah	–
Margat	al-Marqab	–
Mirabel	Mijdal Afiq	–
Mont Ferrand	Ba'rin	–
Montfort	Qal'at al-Qurayn	–
Montréal (Krak de Montréal)	Shawbak	
Nephin	Anafah	–
Ranculat	Qal'at al-Rum	–
Ravendel	Rawanda	Ravanda
Recordane	Khirbat Kardanah	–
Roche de Roussel	Hajar Shuglan	Chilvan Kale
Rochefort	Bourzay	–
Ruad	Arwad	–
Saone	Sahyun	–
Saphet	Safad	Zefat
Selucia Trachea	–	Silifke
Sephorie	Saffuriyah	–
St Simeon	–	Süveydiye
Subeibeh	Qal'at Subayba	–
Toprak	Tal Hamdun	Toprakkale
Tortosa	Tartus	–
Trapesac	Darbsak	–
Turbessel	Tal Bashir	–
Turris Rubea	Burj al-Ahmar	
Turris Salinarum	Tal Tananim	–
Vadum Jacob	Jisr Ya'kub	Gesher Benot Ya'acov
Villejargon	'Arqah	–

Turkey

The northern regions of the County of Edessa and the Principality of Antioch covered part of what are now the Turkish provinces of Antakya (also called the Hatay), Adana, Maras, Gaziantep, Adiyaman and Urfa. Within this rugged and rather underdeveloped territory the easiest Crusader fortifications to reach are the Citadel of Antioch (Antakya) itself, the Citadel of Edessa (Urfa) which, like the walls of the city, contains very little Crusader work, and the castle of Baghras which, though rebuilt by the Byzantines in 968, is now largely Crusader and Armenian. Other castles that are more difficult to reach are Ravendel (Ravanda) and Haruniya, though both of these are largely Islamic rather than Crusader.

Syria

Generally speaking the Crusader castles of Syria are more numerous and easier to reach. The largest and most dramatic are Saone (Sahyun), Margat (al-Marqab) and Crac des Chevaliers (Hisn al-Akrad), all of which have been opened up and developed for tourists. However, Margat and Crac both largely date from the 13th century with later Islamic additions. Fortunately this development has been done in such a way that the castles themselves have neither been spoiled nor over-restored. Amongst the more difficult to reach, but still worthwhile, is Bourzay, which was probably the Rochefort of the Crusaders, standing in a wonderfully dramatic location overlooking the northern part of the Orontes valley. The citadel of Apamea (Afamiyah) is similarly dramatic, though located on the lower eastern side of the Orontes valley. It also has the advantage of not having been turned into an uninhabited archaeological site or architectural relic. The old town still fills most of the area within the city walls while the main or newer part of the town stands where the outer and lower suburbs of the medieval town once stood. In terms of its fortifications, however, most of what can now be seen at Apamea dates from after the earthquakes of the mid-12th century and is therefore Islamic.

Lebanon

The Crusader castles and fortified cities of Lebanon have become accessible once again since peace returned to the area. The citadel of Tripoli (Trablus) includes both 12th and 13th-century Crusader work, as well as fragments of the previous 11th-century Islamic palace-fortress. It is in a good state of repair though its external appearance is more Ottoman than medieval. Gibelet (Jubayl) and the southern coastal cities like Sidon (Saida) and Tyre (Sur) similarly include both Crusader and later Islamic work. It is certainly possible to visit the latter two, and the effort is worthwhile because so much remains from the Crusader period; however, southern Lebanon, though theoretically open to visitors, remains rather tense at the time of writing. In the very north of Lebanon the small but dramatic castle of Gibelcar ('Akkar) is again well worth visiting. However, it remains difficult to reach not only in terms of roads to the site but in a very strenuous climb (without a path) to enter the castle itself. At the other end of the country, in the deep south, the castle of Belfort (Qal'at al-Shaqif) again includes identifiable 12th-century structures.

Israel and the Palestinian territories

Further south in Israel and the Palestinian autonomous areas, many castles and fortifications dating from the Crusader period have been excavated and restored to such an extent that they resemble historical theme parks. None of the Crusader-period walls of Jerusalem survive to their original height, and most of today's city walls were rebuilt under the sway of the Ottoman Empire. In the Citadel, Crusader elements that survived the destruction of 1239 can be found in the talus, the eastern tower, the eastern curtain-wall (including the remains of stables), a postern gate, the base of the south-western tower (again including stables), the southern postern, the western gateway, the north-western curtain (including the lower parts of some arrow slits), and the

ABOVE TOP Very little remains of the 12th-century castle at Kadmos (Qadmus) in the Syrian coastal mountains. Though normally regarded as an Isma'ili or 'Assassin' stronghold, it was built by the Crusaders earlier in the 12th century before being taken by the so-called 'Assassins'.

ABOVE BOTTOM The fortifications of Apamea (Afamiyah or Qal'at al-Mudiq) are some of the most interesting in Syria, and yet are little known. The site formed part of the Crusader Principality of Antioch for a few decades but was then largely overthrown in a series of earthquakes. Much of what can be seen today dates from the reconstructions carried out for subsequent Islamic rulers, though some of the foundations are 12th century.

The castle of Beaufort in Lebanon, as it appeared shortly before World War I. The round tower and talus are Islamic, from after the expulsion of the Crusaders, whereas the walls behind are Crusader fortifications. The oldest part is the rectangular 12th-century donjon on the left. More recently, Beaufort served as a bastion of Lebanese and Palestinian resistance during the Israeli invasions of southern Lebanon. Current restoration work will preserve bunkers from this modern conflict.

north-eastern curtain-wall. Archaeological excavations in the 'Armenian Garden' south of the Citadel have revealed part of the city's western wall including a tower, and a barrel-vaulted cistern that may originally have been underneath a southern part of the royal palace of the kings of Jerusalem.

In addition to the best-known Crusader sites, such as the fully excavated castle at Belvoir overlooking the Jordan valley, and the mixed Crusader and Islamic urban fortifications of the abandoned city of Ascalon, there are many other Crusader fortifications in Israel and the Palestinian territories. Three will be taken as examples. The tower or donjon at Saffuriyah includes ancient and medieval masonry but was considerable altered in later centuries and has been inaccurately restored in more recent years. The remains of another tower-keep have been exposed in Baysan and are still two storeys high. Its enclosure wall is also very unusual because it was surrounded by a water-filled moat – most inland moats in the Middle East being dry. The existence of such a moat was noted by the medieval Arab chronicler Ibn al-Furat, and was confirmed when archaeologists found the remains of freshwater snails. On a rather smaller scale the Templar tower at Khirbat Dustray stands on a cut-to-shape rock base and contained a cistern. A rock-cut courtyard enclosed the tower on its southern and eastern sides with stables containing rock-cut mangers. Other rock-cut features include further courtyards, reservoirs, mangers and cisterns.

Jordan

Jordan has perhaps the greatest variety of different sorts of 12th-century Crusader fortifications, with the notable exception of a walled Crusader city. The cave-fortress of La Cave de Sueth ('Ain al-Habis) in the north of Jordan has already been described. In the south the existing fortifications of the town of Kerak date from the post-Crusader, Ayyubid or Mamluk centuries. The castle of Kerak, however, is on a steep promontory separated from the town by a rock-cut ditch 30m wide. Again many of the visible fortifications were built after the Crusader castle had been taken by Saladin, but the interior contains many Crusader structures. There are now believed to have been two main phases of construction under Crusader occupation in the 12th century. The first consisted of a castle built around 1142. At this time there also seems to have been a local or indigenous Christian monastery at the eastern end of the site, beneath what are now the ruins of a Mamluk *madrasa* or Islamic school. A second phase of building in the late-1160s doubled the size of the castle by adding a new outer wall and huge glacis. This was probably done around the time the Latin Catholic or Crusader metropolitan see (a centre of local ecclesiastical administration) was transferred from Shaubak to Kerak. Shawbak was modified around the same time, but most of what can now be seen there dates from the late-13th-century Mamluk period. Earlier Crusader structures are encased within this later fortress and seem to indicate that the 12th-century Crusader castle of Montréal (Shawbak) was not particularly strong. It may only have consisted of a donjon. Very little remains of the Crusader castle at Tafila, between Shawbak and Kerak, other than some foundations beneath a much later rectangular Ottoman fort.

Petra in the deep south of Jordan is the most important archaeological and tourist site in the country, and is surely one of the most astonishing places in

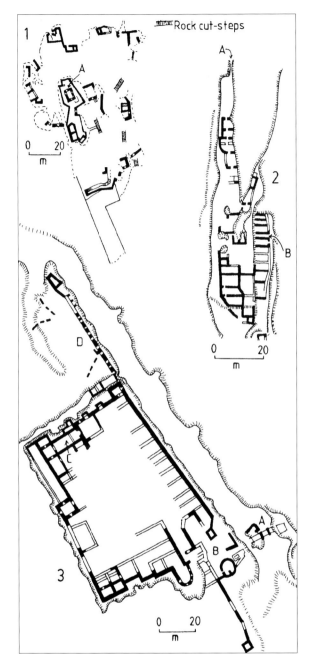

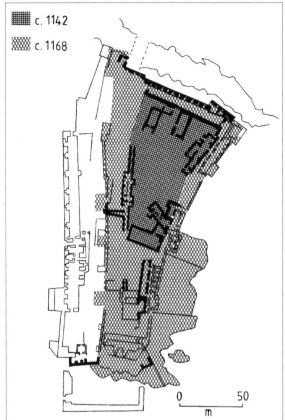

ABOVE Krak des Moabites (al-Karak, after Deschamps & Ellenblum).

LEFT Castles in the Petra area.
1. Celle (al-Habis): (A) donjon (after Hammond).
2. Hormuz (al-Naqa II): (A) southern entrance, (B) northern entrance (after Hübner and Künne).
3. Le Vaux Moise (al-Wu'aira): (A) outer gate, (B) barbican, (C) chapel, (D) ravelin (after Musil)

the world. So perhaps it is not suprising that few visitors to Petra make a detour to look at the remains of three Crusader castles, which consist of little more than tumbled rocks. On the other hand al-Wu'aira (Le Vaux Moise) is worth the effort. It dominates the eastern summit of al-Wu'aira ridge overlooking the al-Wu'aira gorge. Al-Habis (Celle) consists of the tumbledown remains of a small castle and tower on a rocky height overlooking the centre of ancient Petra. The third recently identified Crusader castle at al-Naq'a is, unfortunately, very difficult to reach without specialised transport and a knowledgeable guide.

Further reading

Boaz, A. 'Bet Shean, Crusader Fortress – Area Z', *Excavations and Surveys in Israel*, IX (1989-90) 129.

Brown, R.M. 'A 12th century A.D. Sequence from Southern Transjordan; Crusader and Ayyubid Occupation at El-Wueira', *Annual of the Department of Antiquities of Jordan*, XXXI (1987) 267–287.

Chevedden, P.E. 'Fortification and the Development of Defensive Planning in the Latin East', in D. Kagay and L.J.A. Villalon (eds.) *The Circle of War in the Middle Ages* (Woodbridge 1999) 33–43.

Cohen, A. 'The Walls of Jerusalem', in C.E. Bosworth (ed.) *Essays in Honor of Bernard Lewis; The Islamic World from Classical to Modern Times* (Princeton 1989) 467–477.

Deschamps, P. 'Deux Positions Stratégiques des croisés à l'Est du Jourdain: Ahamant et el Habis', *Revues Historiques*, CLXXII (1933) 42–57.

Edbury, P.W. 'Castles, towns and rural settlements in the Crusader kingdom', *Medieval Archaeology*, XLII (1998) 191–193.

Ellenblum, R. 'Frankish and Muslim Siege Warfare and the construction of Frankish concentric castles', in M. Balard (ed.) *Die Gesta per Francos* (Aldershot 2001) 187–198.

Ellenblum, R. 'Three generations of Frankish castle-building in the Latin Kingdom of Jerusalem', in M. Balard (ed.) *Autour de la Première Croisade* (Paris 1996) 517–551.

Fedden, R. *Crusader castles, a brief study in the military architecture of the Crusades* (London, 1950).

Harper, R.P. 'Belmont Castle (Suba) – 1987', *Excavations and Surveys in Israel*, CII–VIII (1988–89) 13–14.

Jawish, H. *Krak des Chevaliers und die Kreuzfahrer* (Damascus, 1999).

Kennedy, H. *Crusader Castles* (Cambridge, 1994).

Kloner, A. 'Bet Govrin: Crusader Church and Fortifications', *Explorations and Surveys in Israel*, II (1983) 12–13.

Lindner, M. 'Search for Medieval Hormuz: The Lost Crusader Fortress of Petra', *Occident & Orient* (Amman, December 1999) 59–61.

Marino, L. (ed.) *La fabbrica dei Castelli Crociati in Terra Santa* (Florence, 1997).

Molin, K. 'The non-military functions of Crusader fortifications, 1187–circa 1380', *Journal of Medieval History*, XXIII (1997) 367–388.

Molin, K. *Unknown Crusader Castles* (London, 2001).

Morray, D. 'Then and Now: A Medieval Visit to the Castle of al-Rawandan Recalled', *Anatolian Studies*, XLIII (1993) 137–142.

Müller-Wiener, W. *Castles of the Crusaders* (London, 1966).

Nicolle, D. 'Ain al Habis. The Cave de Sueth', *Archéologie Médiévale*, XVIII (1988) 113–128.

Pringle, D. *Fortification and Settlement in Crusader Palestine* (reprints, Aldershot, 2000).

Pringle, D. *Secular Buildings in the Crusader Kingdom of Jerusalem; An Archaeological Gazetteer* (Cambridge, 1997).

Pringle, D. *The Red Tower (al Burj al Ahmar): Settlement on the Plain of Sharon at the time of the Crusades and Mamluks.* British School of Archaeology Monographs, Series 1 (London, 1986).

Pringle, D. and De Meulemeester, J. *The Castle of al-Karak, Jordan* (Namur, 2000).

Pringle, D. and Harper, R. *Belmont Castle, the Excavation of a Crusader Stronghold in the Kingdom of Jerusalem*, British Academy Monographs in Archaeology 10 (Oxford, 2000).

Roll, I. 'Medieval Apollonia – Arsuf; A Fortified Coastal Town in the Levant of the Early Muslim and Crusader Periods', in M. Balard (ed.) *Autour de la Première Croisade* (Paris, 1996) 595–606.

Saade, G. 'Le Chateau de Bourzey: Fortresses Oubliées', *Annales Archéologiques de Syria*, VI (1956) 139–162.

Smail, R.C. 'Crusaders' Castles in the Twelfth Century', *Cambridge Historical Journal*, X (1950–52) 133–149.

Glossary

ablaq Middle Eastern tradition of architectural decoration combining different coloured stone, usually black basalt and white limestone.

antemurabilus Second or outer walls.

ashlar Stone cut into rectangular blocks and laid in regular rows.

bailey, bailli Fortified enclosure.

balista A crossbow, usually of a large form.

barbican Outer defensive enclosure of a castle or city, usually outside a gate.

barrel vault Vaulting in the form of an elongated arch.

bastion Projecting or additional part of a fortification.

bezant High-value Byzantine currency.

bovaria A farmstead or animal pen, sometimes fortified.

castrum (pl. castra) A fortified enclosure, usually rectangular.

châtelain Commander of a castle.

chemin de ronde A raised walkway around the circuit or curtain-walls of a fortified place.

concentric castle A fortification with two or more circuit walls.

corbel A stone bracket to support another structure above.

counter-fort, counter-tower A fortification, usually small, to blockade or isolate another fortification.

crenellation Tooth-like projections along the top of a fortified wall to provide protection for the defenders as well as spaces through which they can observe or shoot.

cubit An unclear unit of measure, about half a metre.

curtain-wall A continuous defensive wall around a fortified location.

donjon The main tower of a fortified location, or a single isolated tower.

double-castrum A fortified enclosure with two concentric defensive walls.

drawbridge An entrance bridge, usually over a moat, which can be raised out of position, usually also blocking the gate behind.

église-donjon A fortified church.

embossed masonry Blocks of stone in which the centre is left raised and usually roughly cut.

embrasure An opening in a fortified wall, tower, crenellation or other structure through which the defenders can shoot.

enceinte A curtain-wall.

forewalls Additional defensive walls in front of the main defensive walls and towers.

fosse A defensive ditch.

gallery A passage, usually within a defensive wall, sometimes with embrasures through which defenders can observe or shoot.

glacis A smooth open slope leading up to the base of a fortified wall.

grange A building to store agricultural produce, usually from a specific feudal fief.

hoarding A wooden structure in the form of a gallery mounted on top of, and also ahead of, a defensive wall.

keep The main tower of a fortified position (see also *donjon*).

machicolation An overhanging structure above a tower or fortified wall, through which arrows could be shot or missiles dropped.

mangonel A stone-throwing siege weapon based upon the beamsling principle, either man powered or counterweight powered.

march A frontier province with a primary military-defensive function.

masonry marks A symbol or design scratched or simply carved into a piece of masonry to identify the stone-mason who had cut the stone in question.

merlons Raised pieces of masonry forming a crenellation.

moat A ditch or fosse forming an obstruction outside a defensive wall, sometimes (but not necessarily) filled with water.

motte and bailey A castle consisting of a tower on a small man-made hill (motte), with an outer fortified enclosure (bailey).

palatinate An autonomous or semi-autonomous province, often under ecclesiastical control.

portcullis A grid-like gate of iron, or iron and wood, usually raised and lowered into position inside a gateway.

posterns Small doors or gates in the defences of a fortified position.

presidium, praesidium A defended place.

redoubt An outwork of a fortified place.

salient towers Towers thrust forward from a fortified wall.

sénéchal A senior medieval military official in charge of inspections of the King's castles.

slot machicolation An aperture or broad groove down the face of a tower or fortified wall, through which arrows could be shot or missiles dropped.

spur-castle A castle built on a spur or promontory, usually on the side of a hill.

talus An additional sloping front along the lower part of a wall and tower.

undercroft The lowest chamber of a multi-storey building or structure.

ward An open area surrounded by a curtain-wall.

Index

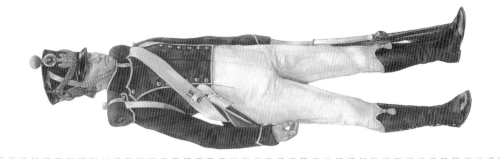 

OSPREY
PUBLISHING

FIND OUT MORE ABOUT OSPREY

❑ Please send me the latest listing of Osprey's publications

❑ I would like to subscribe to Osprey's e-mail newsletter

Title / rank

Name

Address

City / county

Postcode / zip   state / country

e-mail

FOR

I am interested in:

❑ Ancient world
❑ Medieval world
❑ 16th century
❑ 17th century
❑ 18th century
❑ Napoleonic
❑ 19th century

❑ American Civil War
❑ World War 1
❑ World War 2
❑ Modern warfare
❑ Military aviation
❑ Naval warfare

Please send to:

USA & Canada:
Osprey Direct USA, c/o MBI Publishing, P.O. Box 1,
729 Prospect Avenue, Osceola, WI 54020

UK, Europe and rest of world:
Osprey Direct UK, P.O. Box 140, Wellingborough,
Northants, NN8 2FA, United Kingdom

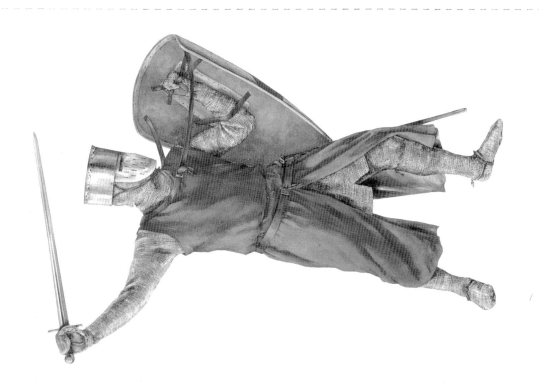

OSPREY
PUBLISHING

www.ospreypublishing.com

call our telephone hotline
for a free information pack

USA & Canada: 1-800-826-6600
UK, Europe and rest of world call:
+44 (0) 1933 443 863

Young Guardsman
Figure taken from *Warrior 22:
Imperial Guardsman 1799–1815*
Published by Osprey
Illustrated by Richard Hook

Knight, c.1190
Figure taken from *Warrior 1: Norman Knight 950 – 1204 AD*
Published by Osprey
Illustrated by Christa Hook

POSTCARD